This book is full of pier  llower of Jesus must ask. And vision and radical call to actic

— RON SIDER, president, Evangelicals for Social Action

All of us who are citizens of the richest nation in the history of the human race would be wise to think long and hard about what we have been given, and what is expected of us in return. Jonathan Wilson-Hartgrove's new book, *God's Economy*, is a gentle yet challenging guide in that vital process.

— BRIAN MCLAREN, author/activist (brianmclaren.net)

Most of the compelling books I know of in current Christian literature are so because they dare to deal simply and directly with radical concepts that have become immobilized by shrewdly nuanced ideas and rampant cultural theology. Wilson-Hartgrove is a master of the art of that kind of truth-telling, and there can be no doubt but that *God's Economy* is a compelling book.

— PHYLLIS TICKLE, author, *The Great Emergence*

Through an examination of money-changing activities ranging from panhandlers to war, *God's Economy* challenges the reader to confront Christ's "For where your *treasure* is, there your heart will be also." A must read for individuals and groups looking to invest time wisely.

— MATTHEW SLEETH, author of *Serve God, Save The Planet,* and executive director, Blessed Earth

This is how the Gospel must hit the ground—running! *God's Economy* is very brilliant, very timely, and very readable at the same time. This is practical theology and spirituality at its best!

— RICHARD ROHR, O.F.M., Center for Action and Contemplation, Albuquerque, New Mexico

This is not the book to read unless you're looking to change your life—in subtle ways and maybe great ones.

— BILL MCKIBBEN, author, *Deep Economy*

Also by Jonathan Wilson-Hartgrove

Mirror to the Church
(with Emmanuel Katongole)

Becoming the Answer to Our Prayers
(with Shane Claiborne)

New Monasticism:
What It Has to Say to Today's Church

Free to Be Bound:
Church beyond the Color Line

God's Economy

Redefining the
Health & Wealth Gospel

Jonathan
Wilson-Hartgrove

ZONDERVAN.com/
AUTHORTRACKER
follow your favorite authors

ZONDERVAN

God's Economy
Copyright © 2009 by Jonathan Wilson-Hartgrove

This title is also available as a Zondervan ebook.
Visit www.zondervan.com/ebooks.

This title is also available in a Zondervan audio edition.
Visit www.zondervan.fm.

Requests for information should be addressed to:
Zondervan, *Grand Rapids, Michigan 49530*

Library of Congress Cataloging-in-Publication Data

Wilson-Hartgrove, Jonathan, 1980 –
    God's economy : redefining the health and wealth gospel / Jonathan
Wilson-Hartgrove.
        p. cm.
    Includes bibliographical references.
    ISBN 978-0-310-29337-8
    1. Contentment – Religious aspects – Christianity. 2. Wealth – Religious
aspects – Christianity. 3. Christian life. I. Title.
BV4647.C7W55   2009
261.08'5 – dc22   2009018609

Published in association with the literary agency of Daniel Literary Group, LLC,
1701 Kingsbury Drive, Suite 100, Nashville, TN 37215.

Interior design by Beth Shagene

Printed in the United States of America

09 10 11 12 13 14 • 21 20 19 18 17 16 15 14 13 12 11 10 9 8 7 6 5 4 3 2 1

For Grandma Ann

Contents

Foreword

One of the supreme ironies of American life is that the society that has talked and written most about the fulfillment of the self shows the least evidence of it. People obsessed with the cultivation of the self, the good life, the abundant life, have little to show for it but a cult of selfishness. The highest standard of living in the world has produced a bumper crop of obesity, anxiety, boredom, and meanness. Happily, there are numerous exceptions; still, the generalization is plausible. Our world is splendidly filled with glorious things and a glorious gospel but is appallingly lacking persons who celebrate these glories with passion and share them with compassion. We are not the first to live like this. Augustine looked at the world around him and acerbically observed that his parishioners were "more pained if their villa is poor than if their life is bad."

Jonathan Wilson-Hartgrove has something to say about this. He writes out of the context of actual American communities that deliberately set themselves against a society that is impoverished by money — rich and poor alike — and discerningly observes what takes place, and has been taking place all over the world, among people who live on God's economy, the abundant life that Jesus promised, an economy of prosperity.

His way of writing is through storytelling. He tells stories. And he is a magnificent storyteller. We are not handed statistics to evaluate or ideas to ponder or goals to pursue, but actual persons who embrace "true prosperity," the abundant economy. The stories carry the good news. Woven into the stories are strands of theological discernment, trenchant Scriptural exegesis, and cultural analysis. He writes engagingly about "extending the beloved community that God invites us into and remembering what's at its heart — the radical abundance of a Father who loves without limit and gives without calculating the cost."

The compelling element in these pages is the author's detailed immersion in the generosity of a way of life that develops when money is dethroned from the controlling center of our lives, and the community is taken seriously as the place of abundance, the good life, a life of hospitality. There are no angry denunciations of the rich or the powerful or of government corruption. He works from the ground up, inviting our participation in the "thousands of small acts on the margins" that add up to a life of prosperity. This is no prophetic jeremiad. Nor is it a romantic-spiritual fantasy of an economic utopia. Jonathan Wilson-Hartgrove is bearing witness; he has been living for years what he now writes. Trust him. I trust him.

The Christian community so needs this witness, for we are all in perpetual danger of money. The American church seems to be particularly at risk as a secularized consumer mentality conditions us to evaluate our Christian life in terms of what we get out of it and as celebrity preachers vaunt money, money, and more money as God's will for our lives. Not that money is immoral or evil in itself, but the words of Jesus and the experience of Christians everywhere leave no room for doubt that money is the most powerful and destructive idol around. More often than not it is an idol that doesn't look like an idol. The demons seem to take particular delight in using money to create believable illusions of good things, truly godly ambitions, and yes, even the favor of God.

Money is everybody's problem: rich and poor alike, Christian and non-Christian alike. There is no escaping money. If we think of and deal with money on the terms offered by the American economy, we will almost certainly diminish, if not downright ruin, our lives and the lives of those around us. But there is a way of unmasking the demonic power of money by setting our imaginations free from the captivity of money so that we are free to enjoy the extravagant economy of God. *God's Economy* is a timely exposé of money's conspiracy to blind us. And it does more: it is an articulate witness that the light of Christ reveals life abundant all around.

EUGENE H. PETERSON
Professor Emeritus of Spiritual Theology
Regent College, Vancouver, B.C.

Author's Note

This is a book for people who have a hunch that life is about more than our possessions, whether we have two dollars in the bank or two million. If you have laid claim to the promise that the righteous will prosper in the earth and you have a Bentley in your four-car garage, I don't suppose I can convince you that God has other plans. I only pray that, like Job, you will stick with God if things go sour and the bank wants the Bentley back.

But if you're not quite satisfied with the prosperity gospel and TV's ideal of success, this is a book for you. It's a celebration of God's economy, where the poor find bread and the rich find healing because we rediscover one another as friends ... and we are not alone anymore. It's a book about abundant life—and I wrote it because I've seen enough *true* abundance that I can't help saying to everyone I meet on my journey, "Hey, listen, this might be what we're all waiting for. Want to come and see?"

CHAPTER 1

Can We Have Our Pie and Eat It Too?

My mom cooked chocolate pies that made grown men use their fingers to lick their plates clean. Her homemade filling cascaded into a hand-pressed crust, and she topped it with meringue whipped into little peaks and browned in the oven. Smelling those pies on a Saturday night taught me the meaning of hope. When she slid a warm, heavy pie onto the kitchen counter to cool, Mom would say to my older brother and me, "Don't touch those pies, boys, they're for supper after church tomorrow." We were to infer that good things come to those who wait and that patience is a virtue.

But sometime in our early teens my brother, who never much liked waiting, learned that if he cut a little piece out of those pies *just so* and pushed the filling back together, no one would be the wiser. He generously shared this bit of wisdom with me, and I tried it for myself. Sure enough—we didn't have to wait until Sunday supper to savor a slice of chocolate heaven. With good timing, and nimble fingers, we could have our pie and eat it too.

Growing up as a Christian, I realized that the promise of abundant life was a lot like mom's chocolate pies. Preachers told me about how Jesus made it possible for me to have eternal life after death. But, like my brother, I wasn't very good at waiting. The more I read the Bible, the more I wondered if God ever meant for us to wait until death to really start living. After all, Jesus said, "I came that they may have life, and have it abundantly" (John 10:10 NASB). Maybe God wants us to have abundant life *here* and *now*, I began to think. Maybe we can have our pie and eat it too.

Otherworldly religion isn't getting much airtime these days. When *all* your pie is in the sky, you're on your own when it comes to facing poverty, sickness, loneliness, boredom, or divorce—the very things most of us want God's help with. We want a faith that makes a difference in the real world—we want to know a God who has something to offer here and now, and not just after we die. What most of us really want is to sneak a piece of the proverbial pie and enjoy it now.

Jesus and American Pie

Whether we call it Health and Wealth, Word of Faith, or the Prosperity Gospel, the good news for many in our time boils down to this: God wants to bless his children both spiritually *and* materially in this world. According to a *Time* magazine poll in 2006, 61 percent of Christians in America said they believe God wants them to be prosperous. Nearly a third of those surveyed agreed that if you give your money to God, God will bless you with more money. For some, the formula seems to work. They testify that they have trusted God and received the blessings of their Father in heaven. Sometimes the blessings are small, like a parking spot at the grocery store or relief from a pounding headache. But often they're more significant: a mansion in the suburbs, business opportunities, healing from cancer, or a saved marriage. If "the earth is the Lord's, and everything in it, the world and all who live in it" (Psalm 24:1), such stories make sense.

After all, if God has health and wealth to share, and God is a loving Father, why *wouldn't* he want to bless his children with the good life here and now? If you're not living an abundant life, the prosperity preachers say, it's your fault—you're not living up to your end of the bargain by living a holy life. That may sound harsh, but the emphasis on personal responsibility means each of us has the power to change our situation. If we're poor, we can claim God's promises for abundant life *right now* and start living in God's material blessing.

Even before I was sneaking slices of my mom's chocolate pies, I felt empowered by my religion to dream big and go for the gold. I wasn't sure which testament "God helps those who help themselves" was in, but it was one of my favorite verses. Growing up Southern Baptist in the heyday of the Moral Majority, I set my sights on the White House, convinced that I had a divine appointment to wield America's money and power on behalf of Jesus. I served as a page in the U.S. Senate and was appointed to be a young ambassador to Germany before I finished high school. Everything was flourishing in my young and ambitious — sorry, *abundant* — life.

Then I almost tripped over Jesus.

It happened outside Union Station, in the heart of Washington, D.C. I was on a lunch break from my job in Senator Strom Thurmond's office, and it was a beautiful fall day. Feeling fine in the new suit my parents had bought me to wear to work in our nation's capital, I strolled down to the train station to get some fresh air and grab lunch at the food court.

The station was a tumult of people, taxis, and busses. I'd been in D.C. a few weeks, but I was still just a kid from farm country more used to crowds of Holsteins. The hubbub hypnotized me. As I walked toward the glass doors of the train station, I heard a voice ask if I could spare some change. Looking down, I saw a man sitting at my feet, a Styrofoam cup in his hands. I hadn't noticed him until then, but I immediately remembered that I'd been warned about people like him. I ignored him.

About the time I reached to open the door, I heard another voice — this one inside my head — quoting a verse of Scripture that I'd memorized in Sunday school. "Verily I say unto you, inasmuch as ye did it not to one of the least of these, ye did it not to me" (Matthew 25:45 KJV).

If that Scripture was true, I'd just ignored Jesus! In my rush to run America for my Lord, I'd almost tripped over him. I said to myself, *That's probably not what Jesus meant when he said, "Follow me."*

I did the only thing I could think to do at the time. I ran back to my dorm room, grabbed a Billy Graham tract, wrapped a twenty dollar bill around it, ran back, and put it in the fellow's cup. But eating lunch that day, I knew that I hadn't done enough. Something wasn't working in my simple marriage of Jesus' gospel with the American Dream. That lunch break was the beginning of the end of my political career, not because I only wanted pie in the sky, but because I was hungry for a different kind of pie here and now. I wanted to know what Jesus meant when he promised "abundant life."

Savers, Spenders, and the Dreams that Make Us

There are two kinds of people in the world: savers and spenders. Savers keep a constant eye on the bottom line, always trying to cut costs and put a little more away for the future. Savers savor the latest bank statement or IRA report. Spenders, on the other hand, love to visit car lots and watch QVC. They try to ignore their bank statements but can hardly resist reading every credit card offer they get.

I'm a born saver. Every quarter I ever got as a kid went into a piggy bank, which I picked up after each deposit to feel if it was any heavier. Before my brother and I started school, our grandma opened savings accounts for both of us. I learned to add by penciling my deposits into that little blue book from the Branch Bank & Trust.

Early in high school, before I went off to D.C. and Germany, I decided I wanted to tour Europe on my spring break. My parents said that would be fine, but I had to earn the money myself.

So I started selling candy bars for a dollar between classes. I could get the bars in a variety box for fifty cents each. When I sold a box, I'd deposit half the money in my savings account and reinvest the other half in a new box. After I'd done that a couple of times, I started paying attention to prices. I noticed that the Sam's Club sold candy by the case, or about thirty cents a bar. So I invested a good bit of my savings into a case of each kind and started to pack my own variety box. By the time spring break rolled around, I'd made over two thousand dollars.

I suppose that in the end savers and spenders aren't really all that different. We all spend money to get what we want—it's just the object of our desires, and how long we're willing to wait, that changes. At root, however, most of our desires are just that—*our* desires. We humans are generally a pretty selfish bunch. Even our efforts to help others are often driven by a desire to feel good about ourselves. Money has a way of exposing what our true desires and priorities are.

A deep part of us really *does* want to do good. The trouble is that we're experts at fooling ourselves. That day in D.C. when I ignored Jesus after almost tripping over him, I started to think about what I *really* wanted and what Jesus wanted for me. Part of the dream that was driving me to the White House was a hope that I could help poor people like that homeless man on the street. I wanted to make our economy work so that everyone could have a piece of America's pie. But the dream kept me moving too fast to notice a homeless man. The dream kept me from stopping to see Jesus.

Jesus said, "Where your treasure is, there your heart will be also" (Matthew 6:21). Most of us want our hearts to be set on the things of God. We want to use what we have to make our best dreams happen. But, like me, most of us get off track. We live in an age of incredible wealth, and our treasures have more power than we know. We invest our money and ourselves in things that shape our hearts and our desires. If we're enjoying the "good life," we're likely to miss the abundant life that Jesus wants to give us.

Dreams Interrupted,
Yet Somehow Still True

Sometimes the greatest gift God can give us is to get in the way of our dreams. Genesis tells the story of a young dreamer named Joseph. He had visions of achieving a high office but wasn't shrewd enough to present his ambition in terms of "service." He told his brothers he had a dream that they were gathering wheat in the field when suddenly his pile of wheat stood up on its own and all of theirs bowed down to his. Needless to say, this did not endear him to his older brothers. When they got a chance, Joseph's brothers sold him off to some slave traders and told their father he'd been killed.

The slavers sold Joseph to a man named Potiphar, who was an official in Egypt's royal court. This wasn't how Joseph had envisioned his journey to the halls of power, but he made the best of it. He won the trust of his master, and Potiphar eventually put Joseph in charge of his whole household, but Potiphar's wife wanted to have a little fling with her servant. When Joseph refused, she used her power to send him to prison.

Again, this was not the way Joseph had dreamed it. In prison, however, Joseph met some other dreamers. One had served as cupbearer in the royal court, the other as baker. They weren't having the best of times either, and their dreams were troubling. Joseph said his God had power to interpret dreams, so the cupbearer told his dream to Joseph.

Later, after the cupbearer was restored to his position as Joseph had predicted, Pharaoh was troubled by some dreams of his own. No one knew what they meant, but the cupbearer remembered Joseph's talent for interpretation, and soon Joseph found himself in the unique position of advising the most powerful man in the world.

More specifically, God allowed Joseph to see in Pharaoh's dreams that lean years were coming in an agricultural economy. Thrifty in his own right, Joseph advised storing up grain while the harvest was good so that the coming famine wouldn't be a humanitarian or economic disaster. Pharaoh heeded Joseph's advice, and when events unfolded as predicted, Pharaoh put Joseph in charge of the whole kingdom.

We're tempted to stop reading Joseph's story at this point. If the story ended here, it would make for a good rags-to-riches tale. The young dreamer makes naive mistakes, but struggles through the hard times to realize his dream of ruling a great nation. Part of me wants to read the story that way (and hope that I might still make it to the White House one day!). But to stop here is to miss Jesus.

Joseph soon finds himself in a difficult position. While managing the distribution of grain during the famine, Joseph meets with some men from Canaan he immediately recognizes as his brothers. His childhood dream has come true: his brothers are bowing down to him, begging for grain. But they're more than just his brothers now—they're the guys who betrayed him.

Most of us would rather not confront our dreams so directly. If we're down and out, struggling to make ends meet, we like the story of Joseph in prison. It's encouraging to know that God can make a way when things seem helpless. Joseph's story helps us remain hopeful and press on. If, on the other hand, we're materially successful, we like the story of Joseph serving as Pharaoh's administrator. Joseph's faithful stewardship impresses us, and we like to think the system will run better with God's man in the White House.

But when Joseph confronts his brothers, we are confronted with the demand to be honest about our true desires. Joseph recognizes his brothers as his enemies, but they don't recognize him. He has the power to do with them whatever he wants, and it's clear from the story that he's conflicted, reducing them to weeping and begging more than once. In the end, though, Joseph says to his brothers, "God sent me ahead of you to ... save your lives" (Genesis 45:7). Joseph serves as a type for one who will come after him, loving his enemies and giving himself for the sake of their salvation. Joseph's dream is transformed into Jesus' vision of an abundant life—a life marked less by an abundance of possessions than by abundant relationships.

Living the Dream that Lasts

In the 1960s, after Martin Luther King Jr. told America about his dream, my friend Ann Atwater became a local organizer in Durham, North Carolina's civil rights movement. In Dr. King, Ann saw that the movement was not just about equal opportunity to live the American Dream. It was about a deep personal and social struggle to dream a *new* dream, a dream more concerned with the economy of heaven.

In 1968, Dr. King turned his energy toward the Poor People's Campaign, a national effort to organize for a new kind of economy in America. King was in Memphis to help sanitation workers demand humane treatment and just wages when he was killed April 4, 1968. Forty years after King's death, a young reporter interviewed my friend Ann, who continued to organize and preach the good news of Jesus in her neighborhood after King's assassination. The reporter asked Ann how it felt, forty years after the Poor People's Campaign, to be a poor person in a poor neighborhood.

"What do you mean 'poor'?" Ann replied. "I ain't poor. My Father owns the cattle on a thousand hills, and I have all I need."

The young reporter thought Ann was giving her some old-time otherworldly religion, so her article about a poor black woman's struggle and our society's need for change missed an equally important truth about God's radical abundance.

Although the IRS says Ann has an income below the federal poverty level, her Father's wealth is real in the here and now, a fact that might jar certain prosperity preachers. Ann has more than she needs, and she shares what is given to her freely. For the past forty years, Ann has organized for her community, redistributed resources among neighbors, paid neighbors' light bills, and fed the hungry at her table. When she doesn't have enough to pay her own bills, she has friends who pay them for her. Ann has found her home in a community of true abundance where there isn't a single Bentley.

Unlike many civil rights leaders who have moved up

and out of their neighborhoods, Ann remains. When her neighbors need something, she calls city hall or a friend in the state legislature. She calls, and they listen. When Ann tells them what she wants, she tells them about her Father's dream for a new creation. She tells them about a world where there's enough for everyone's need, not everyone's greed. She extends an invitation: come and be part of the good life that God's economy makes possible.

Ann is not alone. Beyond the flicker of televised Christianity, more and more followers of Jesus refuse to believe that our only choices are pie-in-the-sky poverty and the materialism of the American Dream. There is a third way, God's way of radical abundance in the here and now. This third way requires the transformation of our dreams and desires; it demands a revolution of our imagination.

There is a way to receive *real* abundant life, not the version measured in dollar signs and square footage that ultimately leaves us wanting. Joel Osteen and T. D. Jakes are right about one thing: our God of abundance *does* want to give you your best life now. It's just that God's abundance is more radical than many of us have dared to dream. We sell ourselves short if we think that the joy of the Lord can be captured in a cosmetically whitened smile. Our God offers so much more.

The same God who transformed Joseph's dream into a parable of divine love wants to prepare our imaginations for a new way of life.

CHAPTER 2

Hungry
for More

My son, JaiMichael, loves candy. He mouths the sweet syllables with reverence — *can*-dy — often in a hushed whisper. We never joke about candy in our house; it's far too serious a subject. To JaiMichael, candy is more than the peppermints or chocolate bars that attempt to embody its essence. It is a mystic presence. Candy demands its own "Goodie Bag" in a special place, set apart from everything else in our home. Requesting it requires a litany of special words, and unwrapping it is a ritual unto itself. To my three-year-old son, candy is not just a little treat to enjoy now and again. Candy is a force.

It seems strange to me that my child is fixated on something so insignificant. Stranger still, when he finally gets a piece of candy, he often doesn't finish it. Why can't he see that candy isn't all he makes it out to be?

But then I read the eminently respectable *Wall Street Journal*. Although the ads and articles seem sophisticated, they often make the same assumptions about money that JaiMichael makes about candy. It is serious business. It demands a special place, set apart from other things. Dealing with money requires a special litany and language. Spending it is akin to a religious sacrifice. And, like candy, it leaves us wanting—that new car will only make you happy for so long before you're thinking about the *next* new car. Money too is a force.

In Luke's gospel, Jesus says it like this: "No servant can serve two masters. Either he will hate the one and love the other, or he will be devoted to the one and despise the other. You cannot serve both God and Money" (Luke 16:13). Money, Jesus says, demands our allegiance. It is a master who wants to shape our desires and order our lives. As I watch the power of candy in my son's life, I consider the power of money in my own. Why do I want more money when I have everything I need? Why do I so often fight to get a little bit more when I know there are people dying of hunger?

The other day JaiMichael hopped into my lap with his *Pinocchio* book, and I read about how kindly old

Geppetto makes Pinocchio in his woodshop and then wishes for him to become real. The Blue Fairy comes at night and touches Pinocchio with her wand, and the next morning finds him walking around the shop. But he isn't quite real—not yet. To become real, the Blue Fairy says, he needs to bring his father joy.

On Pinocchio's way to school one morning, he runs into J. Worthington Foulfellow. Not knowing anything about dramatic irony, Pinocchio doesn't suspect that this guy is up to no good. Foulfellow sells him to the wicked coachman for a bag of gold, and the coachman takes Pinocchio to Pleasure Island.

When I turn the storybook to the page about Pleasure Island, JaiMichael's eyes grow wide at the sight of super-sized sweets. He sits up straight and whispers with great intention: "*can*-dy!"

Pleasure Island is decorated with gumdrops and candy canes. The children the coachman brings can eat all they want. They gobble up the goodies, throw mud at each other, and break windows. But they don't realize that the coachman is turning them into donkeys. Pinocchio watches one of his new friends sprout ears and a tail. Then he sees the coachman grab the friend and send him off to work in the salt mines.

Thankfully, Pinocchio's friend Jiminy Cricket warns

him that the very same thing is happening to him. Together, they make a quick escape, swim away from the island, and have a great adventure getting back to kindly old Geppetto. Pinocchio asks for forgiveness, Geppetto embraces him with a love that transforms Pinocchio into a real boy at last, and they live happily ever after.

As JaiMichael flipped eagerly back to the *can*-dy page, I thought about how *Pinocchio* had presented our money problem. Many preachers note (especially during building campaigns) that Jesus talked more about money than almost anything else. But what concerns Jesus about money isn't so much how we should *use it* (though I guarantee he wouldn't have approved of Bentleys or teeth-whitening) as *how it affects our relationship with God.*

In *Pinocchio*, Pleasure Island isn't evil because it has candy canes and gumdrops in it. It's evil because the coachman knows he can use candy to turn boys into donkeys. He doesn't want to give the boys a treat, like JaiMichael's grandparents do when they bring him a lollipop. Instead, he wants to be their master and use them in the salt mines. He wants to turn them into something less than fully human and so enslave them.

We cannot live on bread alone—or pie alone, for that matter—and the same is true of money. No matter how much we have, it doesn't satisfy. "Whoever loves money never has money enough," says the Teacher in Ecclesiastes. "Whoever loves wealth is never satisfied with his income" (5:10). We can't help but hunger for more because, like Pinocchio, we were made to become *real*. Even when we're not sure what we're looking for, something tells us we need to look—that we're not yet all we were made to be. All of us are hungry for something that will satisfy our deepest desire which is, whether we've ever verbalized it, to become fully human —a man or woman in right relationship with others, with the world, and with our creator. As St. Augustine famously prayed, "Our hearts are restless until they find rest in thee."

But hucksters, like the coachman, make a living by exploiting this God-given restlessness. More than willing, we participate in their game. We buy the jeans that promise to make us a little more sexy, the toothpaste that's supposed to make our smiles sparkle, the education that will make our kids a little smarter. Just like on Pleasure Island, the endless pursuit of our twisted desires can distort the image of God in people, transforming us more and more into the selfish asses we're tempted to be. Maybe hell is nothing more than working all day in

Satan's salt mine, hoping for just a little more of what we think we want.

But we were made for something more. Like Pinocchio, we were made to bring our Father joy. The God who created us wants to transform us through love into real people—daughters and sons who live the reality of our Father's abundance. Maybe all our struggles with money are really about coming home to the God who loves us and wants to give us new life here and now. Maybe our biggest problem isn't that we don't have enough money, or that we have too much, but that we don't see money for what it really is.

Spiritual Truth in a Material World

The truth about our spiritual poverty can be hard to see —especially in a culture of conspicuous wealth. As God said to the prophet Samuel, "The Lord does not look at the things human beings look at. People look at the outward appearance, but the Lord looks at the heart" (1 Samuel 16:7 TNIV). Our eyes aren't well trained to see the most important truths about our lives.

When I was working on Capitol Hill, I quickly learned to tell the difference between a senator and a staff worker. I didn't know every senator's name and face, but I learned to know a senator when I saw one. I trained my eyes to notice the haircut, the clothing, the manner, and the gait of someone who had power and who knew it. I was proud of the fact that I knew when to nod and say, "Good morning, Senator," on the elevator or in the halls of the Senate office buildings.

I remember seeing a senator in the hall one day whose name I did know. I had watched him argue on the Senate floor and was impressed by his rhetorical skill. Here was someone who fit my expectations: clean-cut and stately; smart and articulate; committed to lofty ideals and the common good. But this particular time, he was raging. His face glowed red as he cussed out a staffer while marching down the hall like an angry basketball coach chasing a referee. It was a side of the senator that my eyes weren't trained to see.

My encounter with the homeless man outside of Union Station forced me to question the path I was on and my assumptions about money and power. But it wasn't just the disparity between the haves and the have-nots that made me question the economic systems that those of us in power usually take for granted. It was also the spiritual lives of those in charge—the people who have "made it" in the world. As I got to know them, I realized that something was missing in many of their lives.

When I was sixteen, my world was black and white. If Capitol Hill didn't have all the answers, then the truth had to be somewhere else. So I started spending my time with poor folks on the streets. In front of Union Station I hadn't imagined how I could start a conversation with a homeless man. But with some awkward false starts and plenty of grace from new friends, I started to stumble into relationships with people on the streets. "Blessed are you who are poor," Jesus says, "for yours is the kingdom of God" (Luke 6:20). If I wanted to learn the ways of God's kingdom, why not learn them from its rightful heirs? Besides, by that time I was living in Germany as an exchange student and needed to practice my German. Homeless folks forgave my bad grammar, and they almost always had a story to tell.

Listening to the stories of people who lived on the streets, I learned that involuntary poverty is evil. I met a man in Cologne who'd been a barber. Karl and his wife had lived in an apartment over his shop and dreamed of raising a family together. But one day, as he watched from the window of his barber shop, Karl's wife was hit by a car and killed in the street. After her death, his world crumbled around him. Karl drank too much and couldn't get out of bed. Eventually, he lost the apartment and the barber shop. So he was left to do his grieving on the streets. More than a decade later, Karl still cried as he told me the story.

The evil of poverty wasn't just that Karl was destitute. In a modern city at the end of the twentieth century, this homeless man had access to more resources than most people in the world. He could eat three warm and nutritious meals each day, sleep in a shelter at night, and get free medical assistance when he needed it. Though he didn't have as much as I did, Karl's poverty wasn't simply a lack of resources. It was a deeper problem — an issue that went beyond his basic material needs. The real problem was that Karl's poverty deprived him of respect. In a world that values efficiency, health, and power, Karl's poverty made him worthless. It meant that people who had been his clients were now, at best, passersby who tossed a coin into his cup. Most of them just acted like they didn't see him. Poverty was evil because it isolated Karl from the human community.

In the shadow of what was once Europe's largest cathedral, Karl also told me how poverty had ruined his relationship with God. He didn't understand why God could have let such a thing happen to him. Karl knew he wasn't perfect, but he didn't think he was that much worse than most people. He didn't see why he deserved the life he had. Karl wasn't sure whether he believed God existed, but he knew he didn't want anything to do with him.

If the kingdom of heaven belonged to Karl, he sure hadn't heard the news. Karl was disappointed and angry for obvious reasons. He was also trapped in the identity his poverty forced on him. Other people saw him as worthless, and Karl figured they were probably right. Karl was convinced that just a little more money could fix most of his problems. Steady income could have secured him a home and maybe some good counseling, but it's clear that simply having more money wouldn't have "fixed" everything. Karl was just as bound by the power of money as the well-dressed senators in Washington, D.C.; the fact that he didn't have money didn't lessen its influence on his life. Money can—and does—master us, from the powerful to the destitute and everyone in between.

"Give me neither poverty nor riches, but give me only my daily bread," Agur prays in the thirtieth chapter of Proverbs. "Otherwise, I may have too much and disown you and say, 'Who is the Lord?' Or I may become poor and steal, and so dishonor the name of my God." What do we do with the fact that both wealth and poverty can get in the way of our relationship with God and other people? If we strive to become the models of success we can see with our natural eyes, we end up forgetting God and tripping over Jesus. But if we turn the system on its head and romanticize poverty, we deny our real material needs and insult people who live and die in poverty and hunger. Maybe there's more to money than we see at first glance. Wealth and poverty each offer their own temptations, but it seems that money has a way of quietly colonizing our imaginations whether we have it or not. Maybe our vision is bound by a power greater than we've imagined.

Money as a Power

"The horrors of Western civilization," writes Marva Dawn, "have required a closer look at the principalities and powers in order to formulate more realistically an effective Christian ethic for these times."[1] For most of modern history, talk of "principalities and powers" has sounded antiquated and even superstitious. Haven't we moved beyond this irrational and imprecise way of naming the evils we're up against in the world? If plagues aren't the work of demons but rather the result of untreated diseases, maybe we don't need the biblical notion of principalities and powers. Maybe all of our problems can be solved by science, progress, and the enlightened techniques of conflict transformation.

But the horrors of the last hundred years have driven us back to the language of principalities and powers. The Holocaust, Hiroshima and Nagasaki, Cambodia's "killing fields," and the Rwandan genocide have shaken us from the optimistic illusion that people are getting better. It is untenable to view these tragedies as anomalies — minor setbacks in civilization's long march toward progress. The evil is simply too global and systemic. Even our "progress" has resulted in a new set of disturbing realities for many people in the world.

Why is this? In his letter to the Galatians, the apostle Paul is clearly frustrated by a similar breakdown between what the Galatians know to be true and how they are living. In a moment of exasperation, he writes, "You foolish Galatians! Who has bewitched you?" (Galatians 3:1). They're harsh words, but I'm struck by how Paul names the problem. He doesn't just tell the Galatians to shape up. Neither does he say that they are beyond redemption. Paul asks who has deceived them to the point that they are choosing to do things that harm themselves and other people.

It's not a rhetorical question. Paul is trying to name

the principalities and powers that are holding the Galatians captive. If we are going to face our money problem honestly, we'd do well to begin with this diagnosis. "For our struggle is not against flesh and blood, but against the rulers, against the authorities, against the powers of this dark world, and against the spiritual forces of evil in the heavenly realms" (Ephesians 6:12). This isn't an issue of the "right" or "wrong" economic system or political party. We can't demonize the rich or dehumanize the poor. Our money problem brings us face-to-face with the full reality of what we're up against: principalities and powers.

In his book *Planet of Slums*, Mike Davis defines a "slum" as an urban area "characterized by overcrowding, poor or informal housing, inadequate access to safe water and sanitation, and insecurity of tenure." According to Davis, more than a third of the world's urban population lives in these conditions.[2] These are not anomalies, not temporary setbacks. They are the devastating realities of the world we live in, realities that afflict millions more people every year.

The gap between rich and poor is wider than it ever has been, and it's getting wider. But no one denies that it's a huge gap. And no one tries to argue that this kind of poverty doesn't lead to malnutrition, disease, and brain damage in developing children. When I was still a teenager, my church sent me to Venezuela for a summer mission project. Arriving at night, I rode into Caracas with one of our denomination's missionaries. Fascinated by everything, I commented to him that the hillsides covered in thousands of flickering lights were beautiful. He told me I'd have to look again in the daylight. Those hills above the city were *barrios*, communities of makeshift shacks where thousands of people live on less than a dollar a day.

I worked at a sports camp in Venezuela's countryside that summer and got to know some of the kids from those *barrios* who were bussed out by the missionaries for a week of recreation. They were loads of fun ... and they were sneaky little squirts—just like most kids. But when the week was over, they went home to grinding poverty, and I flew home to a welcome party that cost more than their families spent on food for three months.

When I got up for my quiet time each morning, I kept thinking about the gap between me and those kids from the *barrios*. I started to read my Bible with that gap in mind, and I discovered the more than two thousand verses of Scripture that talk about God's concern for the poor. When I shared my discovery with Christian friends, I learned that many shared my concern. The gap didn't exist because people didn't care or didn't read their Bibles. Some thought the best way to close the gap was to encourage development and grow the economy. Others thought injustice was a distribution problem that governments should step in to regulate. On both sides, these weren't just thoughts. People did what they could—sometimes with great sacrifice—to put their ideas into practice. But the gap still exists.

The gap is what made me believe in the principalities and powers. People are rich and people are poor, but no one is satisfied. The poor and dispossessed cry out for justice. The rich and famous aren't as happy as they look on TV. We know that God made us for something better than what we have, but our best efforts don't result in a society where everyone can flourish. The rich are tempted to blame the poor and the poor will blame the rich, but the blame game seems simplistic. Something more is going on. The Bible's language of principalities and powers helps me name just what we're up against.

In his insightful book *Money and Power*, sociologist and theologian Jacques Ellul writes, "In this implacable society where the state uses its power to oppress and money uses its power to possess, God in Jesus Christ calls the Christian to live according to God's will; in other words, to accomplish something truly extraordinary."[3] I'm a firm believer in the principalities and powers, and I still think God invites us to participate in the divine economy by the power of the Holy Spirit. In his analysis of our predicament, Ellul shows how medieval Christianity tried to set up a Christian economic system governed by church law. Failing to acknowledge money as a power, the church set itself up to be possessed by it. "The church was defeated," Ellul said, "because it thought it was possible to Christianize and make morally acceptable what will always be the indomitable adversary."[4]

Reacting against this, many Protestant Christians separated their faith from their money and their business. The church had no business in the marketplace, they thought. It's like mixing ice cream and horse manure: it doesn't hurt the manure, but it sure ruins the ice cream. So many Christians said, "Let the church be the church and the world be the world. We'll be Christians in our hearts and citizens and businesspeople with our bodies."

But as Ellul observed, in this way of dealing with our money problem, "the words of the Bible apply only to ... Christians, and only to their inner lives."[5] Our lives quickly become divided between the spiritual and material, and it's not long before the gospel has little to offer in the present world. Our material lives are still subject to the principalities and powers, and salvation means something like knowing things will be better as soon as we get out of this world. Again, the pie is in the sky when we die.

As I think about Ellul's reading of how the church has tried to negotiate the money problem without recognizing money as a power, I can see these two ways in my own life. Like the medieval church that wanted to sanctify the economic order, I thought I could use America's money and power to bless the whole world. When I began to suspect that this wasn't going to work, I became a reactionary—like a drunk man who, in Luther's memorable phrase, falls off one side of the horse to keep from falling off the other. I embraced homeless folks with a romanticized notion of their spiritual superiority. Maybe they didn't have the wealth of this world, I reasoned, but they had spiritual riches.

But seeing poverty firsthand shook me from my illusions and convinced me that money is a power that works with the devil to steal, kill, and destroy. Powers do not want to be named, which is why Jesus asked demons, "What is your name?" They manipulate and possess people by creating believable illusions. Rich and poor alike, the powers hold our imagination captive.

But, according to Scripture, Jesus' death and resurrection unmasked the powers, allowing us to see them for what they really are. "Having disarmed the powers and authorities, he made a public spectacle of them, triumphing over them by the cross" (Colossians 2:15).

A friend told me a story about a little Christian community he visited in Latin America. These folks lived in a remote area and didn't have much. But they worked hard, shared what they had, and thanked God for the life they'd been given. They told my friend about a time when a band of robbers had come through, demanding money from one of their members. He explained to the robbers that he didn't have much money with him, but that he was a part of a Christian community and shared money with his brothers and sisters. "Come with me," he said to the robbers, "and I will see what I can get for you from the other families." They robbers were so shocked by the man's response that they rode off, leaving him with the little money he'd been ready to give them.

"Perhaps," said my friend, "these folks have figured out what it means to unmask the power of money."

Free for Abundant Life

The prophet Zechariah doesn't mince words about the power of money. Prophesying against exploitative leadership in an economy where people are sold and used, he said about God's people, "Their buyers slaughter them and go unpunished. Those who sell them say, 'Praise the Lord, I am rich'" (Zech.11:5). The demonic power of money, according to the prophet, is that it reduces people to property that can be bought and sold. Then, what's worse, it convinces the oppressors that God has blessed them. "Their own shepherds do not spare them," Zechariah says. Like the coachman in Pinocchio's story, the shepherds who are supposed to care for God's people deceive them, use them, and make them into slaves. But the coachmen and the false prophets are also in bondage, held captive to a power that will ultimately destroy them.

This is the biblical background for Jesus' promise of abundant life to his followers. "I came that they may have life, and have it abundantly," Jesus says in John 10:10. The context of this promise of abundant life is Jesus' teaching on the good shepherd. "I am the good shepherd," Jesus says, in contrast to the false shepherds Zechariah prophesied against. "I know my sheep and my sheep know me—just as the Father knows me and I know the Father—and I lay down my life for the sheep" (John 10:14–15).

Like Pinocchio, we have a Father who knows us and loves us. He wants to share his good life with us, even as deceptive powers are trying to take us captive and bind our imaginations with illusions. But our Father knows the powers we're up against, he knows we can't make it home on our own. And we can't beat the powers at their own game, so our Father sends his Son to unmask them. "I am the good shepherd," Jesus says. "I lay down my life for my sheep."

The radical abundance Jesus invites us into is the economy of a shepherd who lays down his life for his sheep. It is the interruption of every economic system, because it refuses the law of scarcity and insists that the impossible can happen. God's people can survive for forty years on bread that falls out of the sky. Five thousand people can eat their fill and still have leftovers from a meal of two fish and five loaves of bread. God's economy is not a new *system* to be established in the world. It is, instead, the fundamental *truth* of the universe. It is the miracle that keeps us all alive, despite our rebellion against God and selfishness in relating to one another.

God's abundant life is not success as the world defines it. It doesn't mean God wants you to live in a mansion on the hill. Such extravagance is far *less* than what God desires for every person—a restored relationship with our Father and the family that gathers around his welcome table. The abundant life Jesus offers is freedom from the poverty that says some people are worthless and freedom from the wealth that tempts others to forget God.

Beneath the illusions of the power called money, this is our deepest hunger: to know we are loved unconditionally and to know our neighbors in light of that love.

Only God can save us from the power of money; the good news is that God already has. If we will believe, a whole new way of living is possible in God's beloved community. If we will but trust Jesus, we can become real.

CHAPTER 3

Eating at God's Table

God wants abundant life for us. Make no mistake: the system of this broken world is poison. It will tickle our taste buds and make mouth-watering promises, but the world's way of living is still subject to the powers and principalities that want to keep us from real life. When Jesus says we cannot serve both God and Money, he stands at the crossroads. We cannot serve God and Money because they lead in two different directions. As a power, money misdirects our deepest desires and puts us on a path toward death.

But Jesus points to a better way—a road that leads to life. This is the forever-promise of God to his people: *I will lead you in the way of life.* "See, I set before you today life and prosperity, death and destruction," the holy God of Israel says to the Hebrew children. "This day I call heaven and earth as witnesses against you that I have set before you life and death, blessings and curses. Now choose life, so that you and your children may live and that you may love the Lord your God, listen to his voice, and hold fast to him" (Deuteronomy 30:15, 19–20). Jesus identifies himself with this God—the great I Am—when he says in John's gospel, "I am the good shepherd; I know my sheep and my sheep know me" (John 10:14). Because we know Jesus, we know the Father of life. Jesus saves us *from* the way of living that leads to death and *for* abundant life in God's family. This is the good news.

But how do we move from *hearing* the news to *living* the new life? Hearing, after all, isn't sufficient. It's one thing to get a call from someone who says he's happy to inform you that you've won a million-dollar sweepstakes, but that's not the same as getting the check in the mail and cashing it. The news alone is exciting, certainly, but we live in an age of deception. We can't believe everything we hear. We want good news, but we want more than that. We want to experience the new life that the good news promises.

The powers and principalities conspire to frustrate our deepest desires and send us chasing after the opposite of what will truly satisfy us. And we humans are easily frustrated. We want the good life in the here and now, but our desires are unfocused, our imaginations limited, and our wants misplaced. We want abundant life, but we want it on our own terms.

In the neighborhood where I live, people sometimes "flip" a house to make a quick buck. They buy it cheap because it's in bad shape, but rather than fix the structural issues that compromise the house's integrity, they just put some fresh paint on the walls, install a few flashy fixtures, and slap some new vinyl siding on the outside. The house often looks fantastic, but underneath the flash it's still the same old shack.

This is what the powers and principalities conspire to do in our lives. They seek to convince us that Jesus is vinyl siding, a quick-fix for turning our lives around. Christianity becomes a way to clean up and make ourselves look respectable in the eyes of others, while all the while we're still on the path toward death. Christians do business more or less like everyone else, but we do what we do "in God's name." If truly following God's call to abundant life makes Christians into well-adjusted middle-class citizens, it makes you wonder how Jesus ever got himself executed.

The surprising twist in God's story is that the way to real life passes through death. Christ, on the cross, exposes the scheme of the powers and principalities: we spend our lives trying to ignore death, but Jesus confronts death head-on. The abundant life—which is so full and rich that Jesus calls it *eternal*—is in direct opposition to a life that shuffles toward death, step after distracted step. Jesus dramatizes the contradiction by challenging death with the extravagant abundance of his own life given willingly to his enemies. Our lurch toward death is interrupted by Jesus' death on the cross.

Most of us don't like to be interrupted. Although we sing songs thanking God for the cross, its actual intrusion into our lives is almost always an offense. Where I grew up in the South, our death-bound way of living manifested itself just fifty years ago in the systematic racism of Jim Crow laws. Looking back, it's easy to see how this system was captive to the principalities and powers and needed to be interrupted. But I grew up going to church with Christian men and women who had defended segregation. They read their Bibles, loved their children, and could be generous—even to people unlike them. But they had a limited imagination in the 1960s. They couldn't see then how the end of Jim Crow could mean anything other than death. It took the power of God and the disruption caused by the civil rights movement to make their blind eyes see.

I've learned a lot from brothers and sisters whose lives interrupted the status quo and pointed toward a more abundant way of life. Among that great cloud of witnesses is Ms. Fannie Lou Hamer. A sharecropper from the Mississippi Delta, she was a poor black woman who suffered the extremes of separate and unequal treatment. When Ms. Hamer heard the gospel preached by a minister from the Southern Christian Leadership Conference, she understood for the first time that she was a child of God and segregation could not take that dignity away from her. She became a singing evangelist of this good news and got involved in the civil rights movement.

In the summer of 1963, Ms. Hamer was arrested for questioning the South's white power structure and taken to the jail in Winona, Mississippi. For almost a week, she was beaten by police officers—beaten until, as she later said, her body was "hard as a bone."[1] But Ms. Hamer was not crushed by this confrontation with death. Andrew Young tells the story of going to bail Ms. Hamer out of jail, knowing the hell she must have suffered. When she came out of the jail in Winona, he recalls, "it was like she had been born again." Young says Ms. Hamer helped him to understand the power of the cross.

For Jesus, the cross isn't simply one event that happens at the end of his life; it is the very shape of his everyday living. Fannie Lou Hamer lived her life the same way. After her beating in the Winona jail, Ms. Hamer said, "It wouldn't solve any problem for me to hate whites just because they hate me. Oh, there's so much hate, only God has kept us Negroes sane."[2] Ms. Hamer had a favorite image for the new way of life she had learned from Jesus. She liked to say that God had prepared a great "welcome table" for all his children. In the abundance of God's economy, he prepares a banquet table where there is more than enough for anyone who wants to come. Everyone is invited to the table, she would say—even Ross Barnett and James O. Eastland—but they'll have to learn some manners.

Learning some manners at God's table: maybe this is the education we need if we want to move from *news* to *new life*. It's not enough to know that Jesus has freed us from the power of death. We want to live the abundant life he promises—to sit at God's welcome table, even if it means interrupting our normal way of doing things. After I tripped over Jesus in front of Union Station, I started praying, "Jesus, please show me your way." Where do we go to get trained in Jesus' way? Maybe what we need most is to sit at God's table and learn some manners.

Learning Manners
at the Lord's Table

Jesus' most extended teaching in John's gospel happens at the dinner table. At the beginning of chapter 13, Jesus sits down with his disciples for a final meal, after sharing life with them for over three years. Five chapters later, he gets up from the table to go pray in an olive grove, but for those five chapters, the disciples learn their manners at the Lord's table. When Jesus wants to show and tell us the way to abundant life, he invites us to sit down at God's banquet.

Meals say much about who we value. It's no accident that Jesus takes the opportunity of sitting at dinner with his disciples to say, "I no longer call you servants, because a servant does not know his master's business. Instead, I have called you friends, for everything that I learned from my Father I have made known to you" (John 15:15).

That sort of intimate sharing happens best around a table, between bites and laughs. Sharing breakfast every morning with my son, I remember little things my mom and dad told me growing up—things they repeated, no doubt, around the little table in our kitchen. But it wasn't just the things they said; it was their patience, their hugs, and their singing that slowly shaped me over the years. So much of what I see when I look at the world depends on what I saw and heard around that table.

John seems to understand this in the way he tells the story of Jesus eating with his friends, giving more attention to the table talk than anything else. The other gospel accounts, Matthew, Mark, and Luke, all record Jesus gathering with his disciples in the upper room for dinner, but only John makes the table the focus. Here Jesus shows us the "full extent of his love" (John 13:1). Here he loves his friends and enemies, stooping to wash *all* the disciples' feet—even Judas's—so we can know what true love looks like. Here Jesus gives his new commandment: "Love one another. As I have loved you, so you must love one another" (John 13:34). Here Jesus offers his prayer for "those who will believe in me ... that all of them may be one, Father, just as you are in me and I am in you" (John 17:20–21).

In the ancient liturgies of the church, Eucharist was the focal point of every worship service, pointing all the prayers and songs and sermons to the table where

Jesus said, "This is my body, broken for you." But the table isn't just important in the church's more liturgical traditions. The little Baptist church where I grew up had a table up front, just below the pulpit. Carved into the wood were Jesus' words: "In Remembrance of Me." Though we didn't often connect them theologically, there was another table outside beneath the picnic shelter where Mama Shirley brought her chicken and dumplings, Mrs. Smith poured homemade lemonade, and my mom laid out her chocolate pies. If ever our little church was one as the Father and Son are one, it was around that picnic table.

In his first letter to the Corinthians, Paul says anything that keeps the church from the unity of the Lord's table is idolatry. It's a strong claim, especially if you've ever been part of a church! Looking back on the history of Israel, Paul recalls how "they all ate the same spiritual food and drank the same spiritual drink; for they drank from the spiritual rock that accompanied them, and that rock was Christ" (10:3–4). God's children were always at the table with Jesus, drinking from the one cup of Christ's life poured out for all. But so many of them failed to *re*member themselves in the one true God. As a direct consequence, Paul says, they were *dis*membered: "their bodies were scattered over the desert" (10:5).

With this history in mind, Paul exhorts the Corinthians to "flee from idolatry" (10:14). This word of caution is rooted deeply in the wisdom of Jesus. Paul knows what we have been trying to remember — that we cannot serve both God and Money. But he also looks back over the story of God's people and tells the truth.

In Robert Frost's poem "The Road Not Taken," the speaker pauses at a fork in the road, struggling to choose his way. Since he is only "one traveler" with one life, he feels "sorry I could not travel both."[3] So it is with us. We are constantly seduced by the principalities and powers to blur the distinction between God and Money — to try to travel both paths at once. But it will not work. "You cannot drink the cup of the Lord and the cup of demons too," Paul says. "You cannot have a part in both the Lord's table and the table of demons" (10:21). We can't because these two tables demand different manners. Eating at them, we learn a way of life from the master of the table. And the way of Jesus is simply incompatible with the way of money.

Paul's words to the Corinthian church are harsh: "When you come together, it is not the Lord's Supper you eat, for as you eat, each of you goes ahead without waiting for anybody else" (11:20–21). Jesus shows us how to come to the table. He takes up the servant's towel and washes the disciples' feet. This is not just a symbolic act. "Now that I, your Lord and Teacher, have washed you feet, you also should wash one another's feet," Jesus says. "I have set you an example that you should do as I have done for you" (John 13:14–15).

Jesus expects us to follow his lead in tending to the basic needs of our brothers and sisters. When we fail to do this in our gathered worship, Paul says, we're not eating at God's table. We're forgetting who we are and what we're called to do in the world. Nowhere is the tragedy of a divided church clearer than a Thanksgiving dinner where some stuff themselves silly and get slap drunk while others wait with distended bellies for the crumbs that never fall far enough for them to get a bite to eat. True, that's the harsh reality in a world where the rich spend more on diets than the poorest of the poor spend on food. But surely that's not what our Father wants for his family. We've hardly begun to imagine the gift of God's economy.

The economic assumptions of our world are clear: resources are limited, and there is only so much food, time, and money to go around. Survival demands that each of us get what we need first. Once we've done that, we may move on to think of others, calculating the best way to manage limited resources.

But the table of our Lord defies this logic. Jesus doesn't assume scarcity, but plenty. He proclaims abundance through seemingly reckless gift giving. Like the adolescent son of a rich man who thinks his daddy's money will never run out, Jesus lavishes his Father's love prodigally. Jesus knows something astounding: he draws his gifts of love from a wellspring that is endless. The table is wide enough for everyone, and everyone is invited. The table is an invitation to enter the relationship of the triune God whose eternal dance of love scandalizes the assumptions of Wall Street and the White House.

Is this just wishful thinking, divorced somehow from the everyday reality of the single mother who chooses between paying her rent and paying her utility bills at the end of every month? Was Jesus just a troubadour, singing beautiful songs about a spiritual reality that doesn't touch the ground in this life?

It's possible. But the poor people I have the privilege to know possess pretty keen crap detectors — if the crowds who flocked to Jesus in occupied Palestine were in any way similar, he would have been laughed into the lake the moment he started spouting pie-in-the-sky idealism. And I know enough rich people to suspect that the authorities in Jerusalem, both Jewish and Roman, would have never gone to the trouble of executing Jesus if his movement had not posed a real threat to their economic system. However strange it may seem to us, safe in our polished pews, the economy Jesus preached and practiced was more than wishful thinking.

So let's try to take Jesus' economic assumptions seriously. What could it possibly mean to base our lives and relationship to money on the assumption of abundance? What difference would it make in our hopes and dreams? In our daily lives? Jesus taught some simple tactics to a community of God's children living under occupation. But before we can pay attention to them, we need to catalog the ways we've been taught to understand Jesus' relationship to economics and power in today's world.

The Available Options

When I was trying to win the White House for Jesus, I had a set of working assumptions about how God wants to order human society. Anyone involved in government knows that people are not perfect; original sin may be the only Christian doctrine for which we have empirical evidence. People in politics know that governments exist to maintain order so that we can flourish in a world full of imperfect people. Without government to check our selfishness, we'd slip into the chaos and carnage of anarchy.

As a young political hopeful in a pluralistic society, I believed in the separation of church and state. I never thought we needed a Christian government. But it did make sense to me that God would call and empower his chosen people to wield a nation's power for the greatest possible good. As a wealthy nation, I thought America was uniquely positioned to steward our resources and lift up the poorer nations of the world—especially those who seemed to face challenges that were no fault of their own. My principle assumption was this: the more control Christians can get, the better. Though none of us is perfect, I figured God could help Christians know how to run things better than anyone else.

But after my time in Washington, I had to wrestle with the many ways power deceives us. What we think is stewardship may, in fact, be greed. The giving patterns of people—both in and out of church—suggest that having more money makes people *less* generous. Though people in power have access to more resources, they are often hesitant to help those in need, afraid that they might lose their place of influence, get distracted from more important matters, or encourage destructive patterns of helplessness among the needy. Though it's not always easy to identify the specific wheres and whys, power does corrupt, diminishing our best intentions.

No one sees this more clearly than the poor. They observe the powerful from a distance and feel the pain of disparity. When poor people cry out for justice, they expose the cracks in our systems of power. I understood our world differently when I became friends with people who lived on the streets and observed society from below. Homeless friends also taught me to mock the power of money by laughing at the absurdities of power —and at myself.

An earnest desire to make a difference got me into politics as a teenager. And when I saw the temptations of power up close, the same impulse made me want to change the system. I learned the traditions of radical democracy and people's movements from the sort of books you find at independent stores in West Philadelphia. And I tried to get involved with "the movement"—mostly by showing up for justice marches and talking to my friends about solidarity with the poor.

I thought this was what Jesus wanted me to do, and I tried to do it prayerfully. I stayed up late at night with friends in our college dorm rooms, reading and rereading Amos and Isaiah on justice and God's dream for the world. When the prophets cried out, their message sounded a lot like the ad hoc social analysis I heard on the streets of Philadelphia. "They sell the righteous for silver, and the needy for a pair of sandals. They trample on the heads of the poor as upon the dust of the ground and deny justice to the oppressed" (Amos 2:6–7). But in the marches we joined, I could never quite sing along when the organizers called through the bullhorn,

> *Gonna go down to the rich man's house*
> *And take back what he stole from me . . .*
> *Now he's under my feet*
> *under my feet*
> *Ain't no system gonna walk all over me*

I noticed at these marches that poor and homeless people didn't say much. They had helped me see the cracks in the "system," but they weren't usually the people with the bullhorns. Others were eager to speak for them, to organize them into a power block. I got to know some of these organizers. They didn't sport the blue blazer I'd worn on Capitol Hill, but they reminded me of me. They desperately wanted to make a difference in the world—and they believed they needed power to do it. I'd thought I would just go on down to the rich man's house, make friends with him, and change things through my positive influence. These folks figured it was best to bang down the front door and throw the rich man out in the street. But the desire was the same: we all wanted to be in charge.

This realization depressed me. "God," I prayed, "what am I supposed to do?" I searched the Scriptures and knew God had a better plan for the world than what I saw happening around me. But how were we ever supposed to get there? How did God want to change the world?

I knew Jesus wasn't just peddling a spiritual tonic to help us make it through this world. Jesus had promised a more abundant life here and now. How were we supposed to get there? Cozying up to the powerful for the sake of influence seemed to re-create us in the image of the powerful. But joining the revolution seemed to do much the same thing in the end. Once you've driven the rich man out of his house, the house is yours, and when the house belongs to you, you're the rich man.

I was stuck. I wasn't going to be able to strike a balance between extremes or bracket my concerns and move on. I desperately wanted to walk the way that leads to life, but my imagination was under occupation. I'd lost my way. Two roads diverged in front of me, and both appeared to be dead ends. I was only one traveler, and I was stuck.

The Way of Tactics

In the prophetic tradition of the black church that Ms. Fannie Lou Hamer embodied, the old folks liked to say, "God can make a way out of no way." When the Hebrew children came down to the Red Sea and turned around to see Pharaoh's army at their back, they couldn't see a way out. They were tempted to despair. Should they surrender and return to slavery in Egypt? Should they throw themselves into the sea and hope for something better after death? What do you do when you're stuck with no way out?

Our imaginations are captivated by the options of the powers and principalities. The way of Jesus, however, is a way we could never imagine. It is the way God makes when there is no way. Jesus was born homeless to a family living under Roman occupation and grew up as a refugee in Egypt because the authorities back home wanted him dead. Jesus had no illusions of changing the world by taking over the palace. He was marginalized from the start.

There were other available options in Jesus' day, but

he rejected them as well. The Pharisees represented otherworldly pie-in-the-sky, but Jesus rejected their way. The Zealots advocated revolution, and while Jesus sympathized with their concerns and even drafted a few of them as his disciples, he refused to take control of Jerusalem by violence. By all accounts, he had the popular support for an overthrow on the first Palm Sunday, and Judas seems to have thought they should go for it. But Jesus chose another way.

All of your familiar options, Jesus says, are dead ends. They won't get you to God's kingdom *because none of them is radical enough.* At God's table, Jesus says, "I am the way ..." (John 14:6a). "Watch me. Just as Israel went all the way to the Red Sea, I will go to the cross." It is at the ultimate dead end that God makes a way out of no way. Jesus rises from the dead.

The resurrection is an invitation for us to reread Jesus' life—to hear again what he tried to teach the disciples about God's abundance. Power is deceptive, and we cannot wield it without being controlled by it. Following the way of Jesus doesn't require us to be in power. When we see the evils of empire, most of us want to end the occupation, and if we can't, we get depressed. The options, it seems, are to compromise with power and do the best we can or drop out of the "system" and stay pure on our own. But Jesus offers us a way to live abundant life when you can't drive the Romans out. He teaches tactics for ushering in a kingdom through the cracks.

Our power-obsession has trained us to imagine Jesus' movement like a global McDonald's. Billions are served, we think, when franchises of a corporate-like structure spread to every city and hamlet, crushing the competition through market dominance. But when we pay attention to the way Jesus organized Palestinian peasants in the first century, his movement looks more like Al-Qaeda than McDonald's. Of course, Jesus rejects violence and his understanding of the world is not just a reaction against the dominant system. But Al-Qaeda might be the analogy we need to jolt us from our addiction to power and control. Proper tactics allow the weak to make a stand and to spread.

We are so steeped in the strategic thinking of the dominant culture that it's hard to even recognize Jesus' tactical imagination. But the visibility of an organization like Al-Qaeda reminds us just how powerful tactics can be. Unified by a common understanding of the world, people can gather in cells, beneath the radar of those in power, to begin living a new way of life in the midst of the world as it is. When those in charge recognize the threat, they may try to wipe the movement out. But it's hard to beat guerilla tactics. When you destroy one cell, three new ones pop up. Because leadership is decentralized, the enemy can't just take out a single commander. If they do, new leaders emerge from the ranks.

It may require fresh imagination to accept the notion that Jesus taught and practiced tactics. But once we do, his simple teachings begin to come to life. What used to sound like wishful thinking or enigmatic religious talk is suddenly practical advice for a path toward the new life that God has already given.

The remainder of this book considers Jesus' tactics for a good life now. Each chapter focuses on a tactic Jesus offered for slipping God's kingdom through a particular crack he could see in this world's system. The tactics only make sense if we see them in light of the resurrection. They are seeds planted in the cracks and crevices, not simply to tear down the brittle structures of the principalities and powers of this age, but also to grow life-giving branches that offer shade to the weary and fruit to the hungry. They are God's way in miniature, pregnant with the new world of restored relationship where lion and lamb lay down together and all is as God made it to be.

Saints and holy fools have been experimenting with these tactics for two millennia now. I want to tell some of their stories, but not as models for a new economic structure. The point of Jesus' tactical imagination is that it *doesn't* try to restructure the world. Maybe Al-Qaeda as a model can help shake us from our strategic thinking. But Al-Qaeda isn't nearly radical enough. In the end, it wants what every broken system wants — the power to control. Unlike all the revolutionaries before or since him, Jesus knows that we'll end up dying in this world's economy whether it is capitalist, socialist, or communist. We don't need to work for a new global economy. We need, instead, to trust the peculiar way of Jesus and believe that God's abundance is already enough. God's table is prepared and ready, overflowing with abundance for anyone who'll come.

The tactics of Jesus have the power to liberate our imaginations and inspire creative subversions of the status quo. They carve out a space where we can ask questions we never knew we could ask:

> What if it's possible to live as citizens of
> God's abundant kingdom no matter
> what government we live under?

What if it's possible to work against the
principalities and powers of this age
without being captive to them ourselves?

What if it's possible to live God's good life
here and now, no matter what economic
situation we find ourselves in?

What if another world is possible?

What if it's already here?

To interrupt the logic of scarcity by trusting Jesus in
our homes, churches, and communities is to proclaim
the only true Economy—the kingdom that has broken
into this world and will one day utterly consume it in a
new heaven and a new earth.

CHAPTER 4

Subversive Service: How God's Economy Slips In

TACTIC #1: *"If anyone wants to be first, he must be the very last, and the servant of all."*
Mark 9:35

Like us, the men and women who populate the New Testament worried every day about the material stuff of life—food, clothing, health, and work. We misread the Bible when we overspiritualize it, assuming that everything Jesus said was about an inner reality or an otherworldly hope. Jesus was born into the real world—a world of Palestinian peasants, powerful religious leaders, and Roman oppressors—and the people he hung around didn't have time to listen to a spiritual guru. Like all of us, they had spiritual needs, but it was hard to ponder their relationship with God when they had to wake up before dawn to work.

Jesus ministered in a real economy, a material world that was every bit as messy and detailed as the one we inhabit when we buy a used car or close a real estate deal. The economy of the first century was different, though, in one important way—it was not based in national and global markets, as ours is, but in households. Economic life centered on the home. The household was the fundamental unit of production, reproduction, cultivation, exchange, and consumption. People met nearly all of their needs at home; even when trade happened on a larger scale, it was not between corporations but household to household.

The Greek roots of our word *economy* reveal something about how people in Jesus' day imagined their material lives. The word comes from *oikos*, which means household or home, and *nomos*, which is the law or established order. In its most basic sense then, an economy is the established order of a household, the material life of exchange that is shared among people who depend on one another in a common way of life.

So when Jesus described the divine economy of God's banquet table, he talked about what home looks like once we're adopted into God's family. In our industrialized world, we've internalized a sharp distinction between the private sphere of the home and the public sphere of commerce and trade, so we're prone to hear much of what Jesus says about the home as instructions about private morality. Family values, however, were not private values in Jesus' world. Familial and economic life were inseparable and happened in the same space.

Jesus' audience had a concrete picture in their minds of what abundant life looked like in this economy. The head of the household—or *pater familias* in Latin—served as an icon for everyone's hopes. He wanted the daily needs of his household met by the labor of servants, children, and wives so that he could have leisure time to enjoy friendship and good conversation. In a world before CEOs, to be the father of a wealthy household was to be all that anyone could be economically. An abundant life was one in which daddy was the self-sufficient king of his own castle. All of that was wrapped up in the role of "father."

Without overlooking the differences between the ancient household and today's global economy, we can recognize some of our contemporary economic assumptions in the ideal of the *pater familias*. Though we're suspicious of patriarchy and don't like the idea of slavery anymore, our dreams of the good life are still rooted deeply in this ancient ideal and its practices. What business woman doesn't dream of the Caribbean vacation when she and her family will be waited on hand and foot? What academic doesn't at least implicitly enjoy the fact that there are other people to mow the lawn, cook the food, and wash the toilets while he enjoys meaningful conversation with up-and-coming professionals? The world has changed its ways of organizing economic life in the past two thousand years, but our desires haven't changed much. Without an alternative economic vision to transform us, we easily buy into this world's economy and its imagination.

Focus on the Family

In the tenth chapter of Mark's gospel, Jesus focuses on the family to teach his disciples how God's economy slips into the world. "People were bringing little children to Jesus to have him touch them," Mark recounts, "but the disciples rebuked them" (10:13). On the face of it, this seems strange. Why would the disciples have such a strong response? People were always crowding Jesus, asking to be blessed and healed. Why did it get under the disciples' skin when some normal folks brought their kids for a blessing? Isn't this the sort of thing that preachers and politicians are supposed to do—shake hands and kiss babies?

Mark offers some background in the chapter before this scene when he tells a story about an argument that the disciples had on the road to Capernaum. Jesus overhears the guys grumbling with one another, and he asks what it's about. They don't want to tell him—they're embarrassed that they've been arguing about who was the greatest among them. They're stuck with the zero-sum assumption that becoming great means making someone else small. In an economy of scarcity, we get used to thinking in terms of competition.

But over and against this economy's way of thinking, Jesus offers his first tactic for abundant life: "If anyone wants to be first, he must be the very last, and the servant of all" (Mark 9:35). If you really want to be great, Jesus says, don't aspire to become the successful father of a great household. Don't worship self-sufficiency and a system where others have to serve for you to achieve the good life of leisure. If you really want abundant life, Jesus tells the disciples, try to become least in the household economy. Make yourself the servant of all.

Mark says Jesus called a child to stand beside him as

he was teaching this tactic. "Whoever welcomes one of these little children in my name welcomes me," Jesus said; "and whoever welcomes me does not welcome me but the one who sent me" (9:37). This is the model that the disciples are rebuking when they send the children away from Jesus in Mark chapter ten. The child whom Jesus stood in their midst represented the very lowest of servants in the household economy, too young and weak to be even as valuable as an adult slave. In the ancient household economy, children were worthless. In God's economy, Jesus said, welcoming the lowest of servants was the same as welcoming the Father—the *pater familias*. But the disciples were having none of it. Dragging Jesus into their argument about who is greatest, they tell the parents pressing around Jesus to take their kids and get lost.

"When Jesus saw this, he was indignant" (10:14). The disciples weren't simply shooing away some kids—they were publicly rejecting the instruction Jesus had recently given them. They didn't want to welcome the least valuable people into the presence of their rabbi. Resources were limited, the disciples thought, and Jesus' time and energy should only be spent on the most promising candidates. After all, the disciples were grown men, capable of running great households of their own someday.

Maybe the disciples figured that when Jesus said, "Follow me," he was offering them access into a higher circle—like the high school senior who imagines a whole world of opportunity when she gets a letter saying, "We are pleased to inform you that you have been accepted into Harvard University." Soon James and John will privately reveal their true desires to Jesus, asking if they might have the top posts in his coming administration (10:37). They want the sort of access you need to become a "great man"—to be the father of an abundant household. The disciples keep thinking God's economy works like the system of this world. They want Jesus to help them get ahead.

But Jesus says, "Let the little children come to me," his voice no doubt still indignant, "and do not hinder them, for the kingdom of God belongs to such as these. I tell you the truth, anyone who will not receive the kingdom of God like a little child will never enter it" (10:14–15). So often we take this verse out of context. In a world where children are often romantically idealized, we're prone to wax eloquent about the virtues of childlike faith or the exuberant joy of a kid on Christmas morning. Simple trust and wonder are great, but they are not what Mark is pointing to. Jesus fires back in the argument about who is greatest by saying that the kingdom he's been teaching them about will be completely closed to them if they don't become weak, despised servants, like children in the household economy.

As repulsive as it might seem to young revolutionaries, Jesus says you don't overthrow the system of this world by beating the rulers at their own game. "You know that those who are regarded as rulers of the Gentiles lord it over them," Jesus says at the conclusion of this exchange with the disciples. "Not so with you. Instead, whoever wants to become great among you must be your servant, and whoever wants to be first must be slave of all" (10:42–44). We don't establish God's new economy by becoming a new *pater familias* and running things right—freeing our slaves, sharing the work, and providing for others beyond our home. Jesus didn't aspire to fix the system or to overthrow it. He submitted himself to people in simple service in order to show us a better way.

Jesus offers this tactic: we usher in a new way by subversively submitting to others in the twisted economy that is all around us. We expose the lie of this world's system by rejecting the greatness that it aspires to and worships. We proclaim the goodness of our Father and his economy when we delight to be his children—utterly dependent on God and one another, the lowliest of servants in God's great Economy of never-ending gift. "I would rather be a gatekeeper in the house of my God," the psalmist sings, "than live the good life in the homes of the wicked" (Psalm 84:10 NLT). We celebrate our abundance in God's economy—and ridicule the false economy of this world—by aspiring to be servants while everyone else is scrambling to get in on the good life.

When I was a student at Eastern College, trying to recover from my political ambitions, Dr. David Black took it upon himself to teach me the way of Jesus. Dr. Black was president of Eastern, and it wasn't in his job description to disciple an undergraduate student. But every few weeks he would meet me early in the morning for breakfast, ask me how things were going, and wrestle local and global issues with me. Near the end of our times together, he would always turn the conversation toward Jesus. He reminded me almost every time we met that Jesus was a man "of no reputation" (Philippians 2:7 KJV). Make this your constant prayer, Dr. Black would say. "What does it mean to be a man of no reputation?" He never answered the question for me, but he lodged it firmly in the back of my mind. What *does* it mean to be a man of no reputation in our reputation-obsessed world?

One summer in college I came back to school early for a student chaplaincy program. To get to know the incoming students, we volunteered to help them move their stuff into the dorms. It was a muggy August day in Philadelphia, and by late morning I was soaked in sweat. As the boxes piled up, I asked myself, "Does one person really need a whole U-Haul trailer full of stuff for a dorm room?" Lugging boxes up the stairs for the fiftieth time, I bumped into a middle-aged man in shorts and a dirty T-shirt. He was breathing heavily and let out a grunt. I peered over my boxes to apologize and saw the man's face — it was Dr. Black.

When I wonder what it means to be a man of no reputation, the image that comes to mind is my college president carrying boxes in a soaked T-shirt, meeting new students as their servant before he was introduced to them as their president. There is no system of the world inside which we can't walk with Jesus in the practice of subversive service.

Even a president can aspire to become the servant of all. If our goal is to climb the ladder — to get to the top and use our influence for good — then we'll always be stuck in a competitive struggle for an elusive power. But if we strive to serve, our opportunities are unlimited. There's always room for someone else to do the dirty work (last time I checked, people weren't fighting for the right to clean toilets anywhere). Whether you're a president or a pauper, Jesus says you can receive the abundant life now, but "anyone who will not receive the kingdom of God like a little child will never enter it" (Mark 10:15).

Tale of a Would-Be Father

Mark follows Jesus' introduction of the servant tactic with the story of a man who wants to know how to find real life. On the face of it, he is an eager seeker, running to Jesus and falling on his knees before him: " 'Good teacher,' he asked, 'What must I do to inherit eternal life?' " (10:17). This man seems to recognize Jesus as master and assumes the servant posture that the disciples have been resisting. But over the course of a brief dialogue, Jesus lays bare the man's true desire: he is a would-be *pater familias*, captivated by the power of money.

"You know the commandments," Jesus says to the seeker. He recounts the second table of the Ten Commandments, the regulations that govern relationships between people in God's family: "Do not murder, do not commit adultery, do not steal, do not give false testimony, do not defraud, honor your father and mother" (10:19). Eternal life—the abundant life with God that starts now and goes on forever—is about living in right relationship with other people, Jesus suggests. Interestingly, he doesn't mention the commandments about living in right relationship with God, perhaps because he knew how easy it is for pious people to separate their God-talk from everyday practice in the material world. Jesus tells the man what he already knows: God wants you to love your neighbor in every act.

"Teacher," the man says in response to the commandments he has no doubt memorized, "all these I have kept since I was a boy" (10:20). We've no reason to suspect that the man is insincere. He is on his knees in the dirt, looking up at Jesus with anxious eyes. He has done everything that he knows to do. He has avoided evil. He has done his duty the best he knows how. But he still has second thoughts, still wonders if there isn't more to life. Perhaps he heard some neighbors talking about this man called Jesus, and he's run to find him, to kneel at the feet of a great teacher and learn the secret of abundant life.

Mark says that "Jesus looked at him and loved him" (10:21). In a sparse gospel that moves quickly and doesn't waste words, this is a striking sentence. Mark wants us to take note. The same tender love that Jesus has for the little children and the other outcasts, he has for this man also. Jesus wants him to join his family. He wants him to enjoy abundant life in a new economy. If only for a brief moment, we see the man through Jesus' eyes. We see a child of God, needy and longing to live the life that he was made for.

"One thing you lack," Jesus says to the man. "Go, sell everything you have and give to the poor, and you will have treasure in heaven. Then come, follow me" (10:21). The man feels a lack, a spiritual poverty even in the midst of a life that looks put together. He can't quite put his finger on it, but he knows it's there. Jesus names the power that has taken him captive without his knowledge—the force that keeps this man from right relationship with his neighbors even when he does everything he can think of to treat them right. He hasn't found real life yet, Jesus says, because he is held captive by money. Let it go, Jesus says, and you'll be free—free to enjoy my Father's abundance.

"At this the man's face fell," Mark records (10:22). The eager eyes that have been fixed on Jesus fall to the ground. The young man is unable to trust the One who loves him. He stands to walk away but knows, as Bob Dylan sang, that he's "gonna have to serve somebody."

We cannot serve both God and Money, and Jesus loves us enough to tell the truth. The truth can hurt. The truth can lay us bare, exposing our real desires and our capacity for self-deception. The man "went away sad," Mark says, "because he had great wealth" (10:22).

Mark waits until the end of the story to tell us that this is a rich man, a well-to-do and respectable father of a sizable household. He is Galilee's equivalent of a successful CEO. The stark contrast between this story and the previous one becomes clear only in the end. Just before the rich man's arrival, Jesus had said, "Let the children come . . . ," inviting the lowest of servants in a household economy to gather around him. It is then a rich man enters the story, exactly the kind of man the disciples aspire to be. They are pleased enough that Jesus chooses them — perhaps because he sees their potential greatness — but they are put off by Jesus' insistence that God's abundance comes only to the least deserving and the most insignificant. No doubt, the disciples are hanging on every word of this exchange between the rich man and Jesus.

Jesus turns to them as the man is walking away and says — can the rich man still hear him? — "How hard it is for the rich to enter the kingdom of God" (10:23). This interruption in Jesus' argument with his disciples has been an object lesson. "Anyone who will not receive the kingdom of God like a little child will never enter it" (10:15). That's the last thing Jesus had said to the disciples before this interruption. Knowing that they haven't missed a word of his conversation with the rich man, Jesus returns to what he was saying about entering God's kingdom—the great Economy that we glimpse at the Lord's table. It's difficult for the rich to receive like a child because riches provide a sense of entitlement and self-worth. It's exceedingly hard for the *pater familias* to become the servant.

In a moment of clarity, the disciples seem to get it. Jesus isn't only challenging the rich man's ambitions—he's talking directly to the disciples too. He's picking up where he left off, trying to make clear what it means to practice a tactic of subversive service to counter the power of money. As long as money determines your desires, Jesus says, you can't have the life I want to give you. Receiving the kingdom means giving up your dreams of heading a leisure-filled household economy. It means renouncing the cutthroat culture of competition that shapes our habits and dreams whether we have money or not. The disciples weren't rich, but they realized that Jesus was talking to them. "Who then can be saved?" they asked each other (10:26).

The rich man who walked away is a reminder of just how much power this world's economy has to shape our desires and our identity. Most of us don't look at our own bank accounts and say, "Wow, I have great wealth!" And if we're honest, we have to admit that, like the disciples, we wish our lives looked just a bit more like the rich man's. According to one study, the average person in America today wants about 40 percent more than what she has. People who make $50,000 per year say they feel like they would have enough if they made $70,000 per year. But when asked, people who make $70,000 per year say they "need" $98,000 to live a good life. No matter how much we have, we always feel like we need a little bit more in this world's economy.[1]

Jesus' first tactic for abundant life subverts the power that this world's economy exercises over us. Jesus says we can break the cycle of always needing a *little bit more* by turning our focus from the rich and famous to the down and out. Don't let the CEOs shape your dreams, Jesus says. Instead, learn from the restaurant waiters and the migrant workers. Turn the whole thing on its head. If you wear yourself out trying to be a better servant than anyone else, you'll soon learn what's true for every one of us: we live by what is given because we are the dependent children of the Giver of all good things.

In many ways, St. Francis of Assisi is the rich young man who did not turn his eyes from Jesus but kept an eager gaze, chasing after the one who said, "Follow me." Francis lived in a time when the economy of the world was changing from the house-based system of Jesus' world to a money-based system of markets and international trade. His father, a cloth merchant, was a member of the emerging middle class who embodied the new economy's ideal of a good life. He traveled to France for business and brought Francis along, introducing him to troubadours and the romantic ideals of an adventurous life chasing this world's pleasures. Francis was, by all accounts, the life of the party among his friends in Assisi. He spent his father's money freely and dreamed of being a knight, winning the undying love of beautiful women, and living it up happily ever after.

But then Francis met a beggar in the market and became convinced that the beggar was Jesus, inviting Francis to serve him. Like the rich man in Mark's story, Francis had it all but still felt like something was missing. He wanted the abundant life that Jesus offered, and Jesus had come to him in the humble disguise of the poor, so he started selling off his father's cloth supplies to give to beggars and rebuild a broken-down church on the outskirts of town. His father failed to see the beauty in this and ultimately brought his rebellious son to trial before the local bishop. (Francis refused to be tried in the legal courts, appealing to God's higher law.)

The bishop acknowledged Francis' good intentions but insisted that stealing was an improper means for charity. In his ruling he instructed Francis to return to his father what he had taken. Always respectful of the church's authority as Christ's body in the world, Francis did as he was told. But he submitted in a way that neither his father nor the bishop anticipated.

"Up to this day I have called Pietro Bernardone father," Francis said, "but now I am the servant of God. Not only the money but everything that can be called his I will restore to my father, even the very clothes he has given me."[2] With that he stripped down to his undergarment and dropped his clothes in a pile at his father's feet. The bishop took off his cloak to cover Francis, and the newly born servant of God walked out into the world, covered in the garment of his Father's house.

Francis' embrace of Lady Poverty is one alternative to the man who had great wealth but went away sad because he couldn't let go of his money to receive the riches of God's kingdom. His story is a reminder that with God all things are possible. But in the context of the disciples' response to Jesus, it is not enough to just tell Francis' story. Because Jesus' challenge to this world's economy isn't just directed toward the rich man. It is for all of us.

The way of Jesus is not just a way of renunciation and downward mobility for rich folks. It is a call to conversion for everyone, inviting us to reimagine our desires and the ways we go about achieving them. Subversive service isn't just a remedy for the rich. It's how God's economy slips into this broken world through the everyday acts of all God's people. As a tactic, it's equally available to those who have next to nothing.

Peter Maurin was the closest thing the church had to the witness of St. Francis in the twentieth century. Inspired by Francis, Maurin taught that "The basis for a Christian economy / is genuine charity and voluntary poverty."[3] He lived much of his life as a wandering beggar and Christian agitator. But Maurin was not the decadent son of an industrial robber baron. Born in 1877, he was the oldest of twenty-two children in a poor French farming family. Maurin was frustrated by the injustices of an economy that crushed people like himself, but he heard good news in the Bible's portrayal of God's economy. He studied the social teachings of the Roman Catholic Church and tried to seek the common good by serving each person as if they were Christ.

In the 1920s, when Maurin was working as a French teacher in the United States, it occurred to him that the practice of subversive service was something he could do right where he was. So he announced to his students that he would no longer receive wages, but offered his services only as a gift. His students could pay him what they thought his teaching was worth. As Kelly Johnson has noted, Maurin "became a beggar in preference to being a commodity.... His poverty was a creative, transformative condition, a way of life to be welcomed and even embraced for the love of God and neighbor."[4] Reimagining his own work as a gift that interrupted normal economic assumptions, Maurin celebrated both the abundance and the vulnerability of the Lord's table. Radical as it was, his tactic of turning his profession into a gift was not a superhuman act—it's the sort of thing anyone can do if convinced that the way to have abundant life is to receive it like a servant.

What God Makes Possible

Saints like Francis of Assisi and Peter Maurin make most of us wonder if they were living in a dream world ...

or if we are. Are we both following the same Jesus? They're like my friend Ann who smiled at the reporter and insisted, "I ain't poor. My Father owns the cattle on a thousand hills." Either she was spouting some sort of otherworldly comfort song or she was privy to a reality that the reporter couldn't comprehend. Most people in the world—Christians included—dismiss or simply ignore such witnesses.

If we take the tactics of Peter Maurin or Ann Atwater seriously, we have to struggle with the challenge of how to rely completely on God in a world where it looks like we have to fend for ourselves to survive. On our own, this is impossible. But with God, all things are possible. Jesus longs for us to live the abundant life that God makes possible here and now.

"We have left everything to follow you!" Peter exclaims in response to Jesus' invitation. The rich man walked away, Peter says, but we're here trying to follow, so show us where this leads—Jesus. What kind of economy does God make possible in this world? " 'I tell you the truth,' Jesus replied, 'no one who has left home or brothers or sisters or mother or father or children or fields for me and the gospel will fail to receive a hundred times as much in this present age (homes, brothers, sisters, mothers, children and fields—and with them, persecutions) and in the age to come, eternal life'" (Mark 10:29–30). If you've walked away from the household economy and its assumptions, Jesus says, then you're invited into an abundance beyond anything you could imagine — a hundred times the resources you had before. And that's only a down payment on what is to come — abundant life that never ends.

But what is this abundance that Jesus is talking about? It's worth noting the concrete economic realities the disciples have walked away from. First on Jesus' list is home. The disciples have already left the economic center of their lives — their trade and all of its connections to a sustaining community. Their siblings, parents, and children are back home, pursing the only way of life they know. And connected to the home in an agrarian economy are the fields, the most important place of production for Palestinian peasants.

The disciples have left an economy that includes all of their most intimate relationships. What they have walked away from is the only real life any of them could imagine. So Peter isn't blowing steam when he says they have left everything to follow Jesus. But this only makes Jesus' promise all the more incredible: you will receive *in this present age* a hundred times what you've left, he says.

Jesus is no less concrete in enumerating the abundance of the new economy that the disciples are to receive. Where they had a home, they will have homes with fields aplenty. Where they had siblings, parents, and children, they will have brothers, sisters, mothers, and children — but notably, no fathers. No heads of household. In this new economy there is only one Father, and his abundance is enough for everyone.

The table of the Lord is already set, and all are invited, Jesus says. You can enjoy this new economy now. An underground network of God's children is springing up, creating spaces for people to flourish even in the midst of this world's broken systems. But, Jesus makes clear, there will be persecution. When the world figures out that we've subverted the status quo, they won't like it. The kingdom party is a good time, but living God's abundance may get you into trouble.

From the resources to the relationships to the troubles we will face, Jesus' hundredfold promise is both real and present. He doesn't say that God will give us a peace that will make us feel like we are a hundred times better off than we had been. He doesn't promise that we'll get our reward some glad morning, when this life is over. Jesus says that those who follow him will receive a new economy here and now. We have access to a global network of people who, with us, have devoted themselves and all the resources at their disposal to the way of subversive service.

Of course, the economy of this world doesn't disappear. We become part of God's economy right in the midst of our world's broken systems, and when the world realizes what's going on, warns Jesus, it will strike back with persecution. Jesus' hundredfold promise is more realistic than any prosperity theology because it acknowledges what we all know—that the world's systems are in rebellion and God's people don't get a free pass on suffering. Abundant life is not an escape from the world's pain. We follow the One who "did not come to be served, but to serve, and to give his life as a ransom for many" (Mark 10:45).

In nineteenth-century America, chattel slavery was a distinctive practice of the dominant economy. Slave traders commodified black flesh and sold bodies on auction blocks, dividing families and denying the humanity of people who were created in the image of God. Many people spoke out, protesting the moral evil of slavery, but it was hard to imagine how it could be changed.

A few slaves like Frederick Douglass were able to save money and purchase their own freedom or even escape from their masters, but this was never going to topple the system. Other slaves like Nat Turner tried to organize armed revolts against the oppressive system of white dominance, but their rebellions were crushed. It seemed as if the economic system based on chattel slavery would never end.

In this midst of all this, while debates went on about the injustice of this economic system and the moral imperative for abolition, a network of people who believed that another way was already possible began to work within, beneath, and against the system, and the Underground Railroad was born. Individuals, families, and churches, many of whom were also calling for abolition, went ahead and opened their doors, arranging for transport from one "station" to the next, often under the cover of night, so that fugitive slaves could escape from plantations in the South to freedom on the other side of the Ohio River. But all along the way, in the little spaces carved out for them by new families, slaves were already free.

When slaves sang "Swing Low, Sweet Chariot," their masters thought they were just pacifying themselves with the hope of a better home in heaven. But they were secretly announcing that a wagon would be passing through that night to pick up those who wanted to flee the plantation. Leaving the economy of their master—the *pater familias* of the plantation—slaves were welcomed into the homes of people they'd never met before.

Suddenly, slaves had family in Tennessee, Kentucky, and Ohio—strangers who were willing to risk their lives for them. They were welcomed into a new economy along with white brothers and sisters. Through someone like Sojourner Truth, they were nurtured by a new mother who lived out the story of Moses, leading her people from bondage to a promised land. The Underground Railroad was a hundred times better than anything they could have imagined on the plantation. It was, indeed, a new life in this world.

But the new economy of the Underground Railroad also involved danger and risk for both black and white participants. In truth, black and white alike were receiving the freedom of their status as children of God. In the eyes of the dominant economy and the law of the land, though, they were criminals. At any point they could be beaten, imprisoned, or even killed. As Jesus had said, they faced persecutions.

But the freedom these former slaves were experiencing hadn't been granted by the world, so the world couldn't take it away. Even if the defenders of a slave economy shot them dead, the former slaves served a

Subversive Service:
How God's Economy Slips In

God who could raise them to new life again. Far from
pacifying the disgruntled masses, the promise of eternal
life gave these subversive Christians courage to work for
a new economy into the midst of the old. A hundred
and fifty years later it's easy to see that theirs was the
truer economy. Legal slavery is gone, but the church of
God goes on.

The Underground Railroad was a movement rooted
deeply in Jesus' vision of God's economy. In our time,
Jesus still offers the tactic of subversive service with the
promise that, if we will trust his way, we will have access to a hundred times the relationships and resources
that are available in our own social networks and bank
accounts. If we believe, we can join this economy now.

God's economy is an interruption of business as
usual. At the beginning of the twenty-first century
we live in a technological era and enjoy the seemingly
limitless innovation of capitalism. No one can deny
that advances over the past one hundred and fifty years
have greatly reduced disease, hunger, and backbreaking
labor. But the biggest obstacle to solving problems like
global poverty is not a lack of know-how, but a lack of
will. It's clear to economists and rock stars alike that we
could end global poverty, but it's almost as if our technology has cast a spell over us. Most of us would rather

listen to our iPods or blog about hunger than cook a meal for people we know and love.

In this context, the tactic of subversive service may look deceptively simple. What difference could it make to serve one person in a forgotten place? We are an increasingly rootless people, moving from place to place and job to job, yet we tell our therapists that we're lonely and wish our lives had more meaning. In a world where so many people are starving for community, this network of relationships that God makes possible through subversive service can be a light shining in the darkness for our homesick souls. The simplest act of hospitality and community-building can help us resist money's totalizing hold.

In Durham, North Carolina, where I live, we have one of the world's best research universities. The best and the brightest come from all over the world to study at Duke University. A friend of mine told me a story about a fellow named John from a promising family up north who came down to study at Duke a few years ago. A sharp and hard-working young man, John had his new laptop and a head full of ambitions, like most young students. He did well in classes and became friends with the daughters and sons of millionaires.

But, for whatever reason, John also went to church

on Sundays. He got to know a family in the church and developed a special affection for them. The feeling was evidently mutual, and the family invited John to live with them. They shared evening meals together and talked about their days. John would pick up the family's school-age daughter after school. He continued with his education, but his friends on campus noticed that his student life had been interrupted. He didn't fit so well into the "work hard, play hard" campus culture. His connection to a family slowed him down. In many of his fellow student's eyes, it limited him. But John chose to spend time with his adoptive family because he felt with them a new kind of freedom.

These kinds of relationships seem simple enough. They happen all the time in the church. But a tactic of subversive service can open our eyes to see how revolutionary this new family may be in John's life. At a time in life when this world's economy is indoctrinating him in self-fulfillment and the excesses of binge drinking and economic greed, he's rushing from class to pick up his new sister at the elementary school. While so many students are exploring a world of ideas without any connection to the place where they live, John is grounded in daily tasks like making dinner and stringing Christmas lights. His adoption into God's family isn't a set of abstract doctrines. It's as real as the new family he shares life with every day.

I doubt John will face life-threatening persecution for grounding himself in a family and his church, but there are real costs to his one small act of resistance to a technological culture that wants to claim his whole life. For John, though, it is unquestionably worth it. And without a million such small acts across our hurting world, there's little hope that the church will ever find the will to use the incredible resources already at its disposal to fight the principalities and powers of this age. But that's exactly the adventure we're invited into. Jesus teaches us to train ourselves in subversive service so that we can begin to make eternal investments.

CHAPTER 5

Eternal Investments:
How God's Children
Plan Ahead

TACTIC #2: *"Store up for*
yourselves treasures in heaven."
Matthew 6:20

When Jim Douglass graduated from college in 1960, his father sent him a life insurance policy as a graduation gift. It was an investment to help protect the future of Jim's young family. Jim wrote his father a letter of thanks, expressing gratitude for the care that the gift represented. But Jim also returned the policy with his letter. He could not accept the gift, he wrote, because he wanted to understand the truth of an "economics of providence" that he had read about in the sixth chapter of Matthew's gospel. Rather than pay the monthly premiums on a life insurance policy, Jim said he would store up treasure in heaven by sending a monthly payment to provide basic care for a little girl in France.

I met Jim in 2003, some forty years after he had begun his experiment with Jesus' tactic of eternal investments. By then he and his wife Shelley had raised seven kids and become icons of the Catholic peace movement in the United States. Their work shaped Vatican II's rejection of nuclear war, inspired peace and justice communities around the world, and testified to the possibility of a nonviolent Christian witness in America. When I asked Jim about my own life as a recent college graduate, Jim always returned to the same thing: an economics of providence. If Leah and I were going to live the life Jesus had for us, Jim said, we had to get this strange economics deep down in our bones.

I don't have the near half-century of experience with eternal investments that Jim and Shelley do, but I've been convinced by our experience and the testimony of others that Jim is right. The greatest obstacle to faith in our time may well be that most of us are too invested in securing our own futures to trust Jesus for the good life he wants to give us now. It's not that we want to reject Jesus. Most of us want more than anything to trust God's abundance. But we are constantly dazzled by earthly treasures and their promise to make the world safe and enjoyable for us.

Most of us believe that if we put away a little each month in savings we can ensure a good education for our children and a comfortable retirement for ourselves. We don't mean to be selfish when we think this way. It just seems reasonable. This is how the world's economy works, even when we take the time to think of others. But in light of Jesus' economics of providence, such economic work and worry seems a bit off. Maybe we don't really trust the abundance of God's economy or the goodness of God's family. Could it be that "responsible" Christian parents should give away all their extra money each month instead of putting it into a college savings account or an IRA?

Strange as it may seem, this is what Jesus' tactic of eternal investments challenges us to do—to entrust all of ourselves and our resources to God's kingdom alone. We can agree with the Marxists when they insist that capitalism is not going to end poverty. But socialism won't end it either. The only real end of poverty was the death of Jesus Christ, who rose again on the third day to make a way for all of us to enter into his Father's house. "In my Father's house are many rooms," Jesus told the disciples (John 14:2). In God's economy there is always enough, and we are invited to participate in God's economy now. We start by investing ourselves in the kingdom Jesus proclaimed and inaugurated. In short, God's children *plan ahead* by investing ourselves *now* in the never-ending kingdom of abundance.

The Power
of Invested Hearts

Jesus' tactic of eternal investments is rooted in a key insight about human nature. "Where your treasure is," Jesus says matter-of-factly, "there your heart will be also" (Matthew 6:21). It may sound simple, but it's an important point: we care about the things we invest in, and the shape of our investments reveals the shape of our hearts.

My brother—the one who likes chocolate pie—loves to hunt deer. No one has to ask him if he does; you can tell by what he invests in. He owns a cabinet full of guns, a camouflage coat, and boots with toe-warmers for cold autumn mornings in a tree stand. He subscribes to *Outdoor World* so he can keep up with the latest in deer hunting. He even has a video camera —complete with night vision—that records his favorite hunting spot around the clock. I'm not making this up. I've watched a video of bucks locking antlers and eating from my brother's corn pile in the middle of the night.

Setting aside his fancy gear and technology, my brother's love for deer hunting is still obvious. Even when he had nothing but a borrowed gun, my brother would get up before dawn and sit perfectly still in the bitter cold, looking for the Big One. Before he had any money to invest in deer hunting, he was *personally* invested. You might say his heart was in it.

We invest in the things we love, and, likewise, our hearts get wrapped around the things we invest in. This is why we talk about the importance of "buy-in" when people commit to things that are difficult. If someone pays for a diet program, they're more likely to stick with it. If we give regularly to our churches, we're more likely to care who the pastoral search committee selects. If you make sacrifices for a relationship, you're more likely to value it. Indeed, marriage counselors often tell people who've grown distant in a relationship to invest more in their partner *before* their feelings change. Put your treasure into it, they say, and your heart will follow.

Of course, it takes some discipline to invest in something before you know how good it will really be. It's always easier to just do what we feel like doing. When we're realistic, this is what we expect people to do. The surprising thing is when people find reason *not* to satisfy their immediate desires or take the path of least resistance. Putting our treasures before our hearts is an anomaly.

The sociologist Max Weber writes that Christianity — particularly Protestant Calvinism — gave rise to modern capitalism because, among other things, it motivated Europeans to restrain their immediate desires and save money, creating the capital that was necessary for investment and economic growth. This "worldly asceticism" combined the discipline of people who could delay gratification for the hope of something better with the social vision of a world that had been redeemed by its Creator. According to Weber, this "Protestant ethic" made it possible for people to put their treasure where they wanted their heart to be and invest in a better future.

It's hard to deny the power of invested hearts to make a real difference in the world. Capitalism has more than doubled life expectancy in developed countries over the past two hundred years. It has contributed to a drastic reduction in preventable disease, illiteracy, and extreme hunger. While globalization has its critics, the poor of the world seem more than ready in most cases to welcome both the job opportunities and consumer products of this economic system.

The logic of personal investment changes my neighborhood as well. In an urban context where many people are enslaved by drug addiction, freedom in Christ often looks like a refusal of the instant relief of narcotics in order to invest in a better future life. Weber is right: faith in Christ makes that kind of restraint possible. It unleashes an incredible power in people's lives. If you've ever watched an addict struggle to get clean, you know there's no greater power in the world than a faith that helps him to invest his treasure in something more than a hit.

The tactics of Jesus don't deny the power of invested hearts. The secret of modern capitalism is a secret that Jesus knew in the first century. But Jesus said it is not enough to deny ourselves so that we can invest in good things. "Do not store up for yourselves treasures on earth, where moth and rust destroy, and where thieves break in and steal" (Matthew 6:19). It's not enough to invest ourselves in a good home, nice things for our kids, better technology, and a stronger military for our nation — *because all those things can be taken away.* Jesus is not saying that a comfy La-Z-Boy or national security are bad things. He's saying they are fragile, limited goods. Since we can't expect them to last, we shouldn't wrap our hearts around them.

That being the case, it's foolish to waste the incredible power of invested hearts on things that are here today, gone tomorrow, especially if God has made it possible for us to invest in something that will last forever. The tactic of eternal investment is Jesus' invitation to unleash the power of invested hearts for the greatest possible good—for God's kingdom here on earth, just as it is in heaven.

But the wisdom of God is often foolishness to us. John's gospel highlights the strange economics of God's kingdom just before Jesus' extended table talk that we looked at in the last chapter. In the twelfth chapter of John, Jesus and the disciples are having dinner with their friends Mary, Martha, and Lazarus. John says the dinner is in Jesus' honor, and he reminds us that this family had plenty of reason to receive Jesus as an honored guest. He had, just a chapter earlier, raised Lazarus from the dead.

But the living presence of a man who'd been dead is not the big news of this story. Here, the focus is on Lazarus' sister, Mary. "Then Mary took about a pint of pure nard, an expensive perfume," John writes. "She poured it on Jesus' feet and wiped his feet with her hair.

And the house was filled with the fragrance of the perfume" (John 12:3). A little later John tells us that this single bottle of perfume was worth a year's wages. It's the sort of thing you're taught to use sparingly, only on special occasions. But Mary pours the whole thing out as a single, extravagant investment. With her offering she insists that nothing is more deserving of her treasure than the body of Jesus.

We know enough of excess in our world today that most of us aren't shocked by a little extravagance. A foot massage with scented oil is a nice treat at the spa—the sort of thing middle-class women enjoy telling their friends about. But judging from the reaction that John records, Mary's act was scandalous.

"Why wasn't this perfume sold and the money given to the poor?" Judas asks indignantly (12:5). Mary's investment doesn't just come off as unwise or a bit over the top. Judas judges it as wrong. It is offensive to his economic sensibility.

Truth be told, Jesus' tactic of eternal investments challenges all of us if we take it seriously. The compassionate conservative might say that a year's wages, if invested well in a small business venture, could create a lifetime of wages for a whole family. A more progressive advocate for the poor might point out that, given technological advances, such a sum of money could easily feed the 30,000 children who will die today from hunger. That being the case, it would only take 365 Marys to eradicate hunger in our world. How could we possibly justify wasting that kind of money on a useless act of adoration?

Jesus told the disciples to leave Mary alone because he knew that she was investing in something eternal — his body that would be raised from death for the life of the world. She was wise because she saw the opportunity to make an eternal investment with the resources at her disposal. Hers was not a "spiritualized" investment. It was as concrete as feet and hair, slippery oil and a pungent fragrance in the room. It was a concrete investment in the kingdom right here on earth. But it wasn't what anyone expected. It was an investment in a kingdom that most people didn't have eyes to see.

There's a story I love about Dorothy Day, who helped start the Catholic Worker Movement. Day devoted herself to the daily practice of "works of mercy" — concrete things like feeding the hungry, visiting prisoners, clothing the naked, caring for the sick. She believed that such simple acts of care were God's good news to the world, no matter how tiny and ineffective they might seem.

Once, when a wealthy woman stopped into the Catholic Worker office to see what was going on, she was so moved by the witness of the community that she took off her very large diamond ring and gave it to Day. Later that afternoon, Day was talking with a poor single mother who lived nearby in a tenement house. Her life was filled with ugliness. Day remembered the beautiful ring in her pocket, pulled it out, and slipped it onto the woman's finger. It was a shockingly extravagant "work of mercy"—the ring could have been sold and invested. But Day's act was an investment in the abundant kingdom of Jesus. Welcoming the poor woman as Christ, Day wanted to bless her with the very best she had.

The gospel doesn't only give us power to delay gratification for better things. It teaches us to want the best things—the good life that never ends. A few years ago, one of my neighbors who is a recovering addict decided to join our church on a mission trip to Mexico. For someone who lives month to month and gets paid by the hour, the decision to take a week off his job to work for free somewhere else was itself a huge investment. But Joe gave himself to the Lord's service and met brothers and sisters in God's family who are even poorer than he is. He says God opened his eyes on that trip.

When we got back from Mexico, Joe told me he'd been saving up for months to buy himself a mattress. But thinking about the folks in Mexico, he decided a comfy bed wasn't as important as he'd thought. He wanted to invest, instead, in starting a "$5-a-Month Club." Joe said people from our church could surely find five dollars each month to share with sister churches in Mexico. Jesus was right: the power of an invested heart can be unleashed to transform our desires and bless the body of Christ—and the world—here and now.

The Greatest Darkness

God interrupts the status quo and opens our eyes to the good life he wants to give us. We don't believe this blindly; we see it in people like Mary and Dorothy Day and my neighbor Joe. But we also know that God's economy is hidden much of the time—maybe most of the time. Our churches and our families are not, for the most part, shining lights when it comes to eternal investments. Where we might expect to find good news—among fellow believers—we often meet disappointment.

For a long time I was confused by the metaphor Jesus presents right after this tactic of eternal investment. It's not immediately clear what this image from ancient anatomy has to do with our treasures or our hearts. "The eye is the lamp of the body," Jesus begins. "If your eyes are good, your whole body will be full of light. But if your eyes are bad, your whole body will be full of darkness. If then the light within you is darkness, how great is that darkness!" (Matthew 6:22–23). So if your eyes are bad, you don't see very well. I get that, but what does it have to do with God's economy?

Jesus seems to drive his main point home in the final statement—"If then the light within you is darkness, how great is that darkness!" You meet the greatest darkness, Jesus seems to be saying, when the thing you thought was light is, perversely, its opposite. We're never in more trouble than when we do the wrong thing thinking it's the right. After I began to understand money as a power, it came clear to me one day what all of this has to do with eternal investments: nothing is worse, Jesus says, than investing in something that won't last and *thinking all the time that it's eternal.* That is how the principalities and powers deceive us—that is the greatest darkness.

When it comes to money, we're never more deceived than when we think we've figured out a formula for getting God to pour out his blessings. In Jesus' day, scholars had studied the Scriptures carefully and tried to figure out what they needed to do to gain God's favor. They knew the Scriptures said there was a way that leads to blessings and a way that leads to curses. More than anything, they wanted to be blessed, and they knew that God's blessing was a material reality.

Rather than trust that God had already blessed them with all they needed, though, these religious leaders turned God's covenant promises into a system for getting ahead. Folks who succeeded were "blessed." Those down on their luck—the sick, the lame, the demon-possessed—were cursed. Not everyone knew the secret to success, but most everyone assumed that this was more or less how the system worked. It's what all their most respected religious teachers taught.

Matthew is careful in his gospel to describe the crowd that gathers around Jesus before his Sermon on the Mount. "People brought to him all who were ill with various diseases, those suffering severe pain, the demon-possessed, those having seizures, and the paralyzed.... Large crowds from Galilee, the Decapolis, Jerusalem, Judea and the region across the Jordan followed him" (Matthew 4:24–25). Jesus has in front of him everyone from miles around who is, in the religious system of his day, clearly cursed. Here are all the losers from the game of winning God's favor, anxious for Jesus to let them in on the secret. In their presence, Jesus does what no religious teacher had ever done before. He says they are blessed.

"Blessed are the poor in spirit ... those who mourn ... the meek ... those who hunger and thirst for righteousness ... the merciful ... the pure in heart ... the peacemakers ... those who are persecuted" (Matthew 5:3–10). In short, blessed are the losers. Jesus doesn't whisper, "Hey listen, here's the secret. Do this and you'll be blessed." Instead, he says to this rag-tag bunch, "You're *already* blessed." Jesus offers his most important teaching in Matthew's gospel to people who've failed at religion. But he's not wasting words. He preaches the Sermon on the Mount to this particular crowd because he seems to have some hope that *they* are the ones who will get what he is saying.

It turns out that religious people are notoriously bad at receiving an economy that is pure gift. I like how Robert Farrar Capon says it: "That, then, is what's really wrong with religion after you've given it all the good marks you can: it rejects God's holy luck and tries to substitute for it our own sticky-fingered control."[1] We hear that God is in the blessing business and we try to get the inside scoop on how to write the best possible grant proposal ... I mean, "prayer request." Or we hear how Jesus healed the sick and we search the Scriptures to find just the right words to make him do it again. We religious people are good at this. It's natural to think that we've earned a thing or two.

We're so good at it, in fact, that we can substitute a religious system for the good news of Jesus. This is why our preachers so often have to remind us that we are saved by grace alone. When it comes to God's economy, we often forget grace (pure gift, that is) and imagine that Jesus is the supreme business consultant or life coach, unlocking for us the secret to success in this world's system. We don't seem to want the free abundance God offers—we want, instead, seven easy steps to a better us.

The real tragedy is this: when this great darkness of religious perfectionism blinds us, our best attempts to invest in God's kingdom become just one more way to store up earthly treasure. When church buildings in the suburbs are turned into family fun centers, complete with big screen TV's and fitness gyms, it's easy to confuse our weekly tithes with membership dues. But the middle-class megachurch isn't the only place where religious people reduce God's gift to the best bargain for your buck.

Eternal Investments:
How God's Children Plan Ahead

Abundant life is just as easily packaged and sold to the poor on an installment plan. Prosperity preachers have built little empires with the last twenty dollars of people who want to believe that God's favor can be purchased for the low-low price of a sincere prayer, a sacrificial gift, or a certain attitude. You don't have to have money to be deceived by its power. Money can blind the poor too, selling them the lie that they can buy into God's great time-share here on earth by doing the simple work of changing their attitude. No wonder Christians have a hard time believing in grace and experiencing the abundance Jesus promised.

But grace in abundance is all God offers. Jesus never preaches a religious system—he invites us into a new economy, free of charge. Anybody is welcome, but we can only live in our Father's house if we acknowledge that our whole life is a gift. This is a fairly straightforward message that Jesus repeated often. It seems like those of us who read our Bibles and go to church every week should be able to get our heads around it. But I'll have to admit that, for me at least, receiving the gift of God's economy has been a challenge.

Growing up Christian during what is perhaps the end of Christendom in America, I became critical of a culturally captive lifestyle that domesticated Jesus like a house cat and generally supported the principalities and powers. Such a religion wasn't just wrong—it was vapid. I wasn't the only person to notice this. Nor was I the first to think that the only hope for the church in this kind of culture is for some people to band together and try to take Christianity seriously as a way of life. To recover from my addiction to money and its desires, I checked into a network of Christian communities.

I've described the communities that I stumbled into as a "new monasticism" in North America, and I'm still convinced that it's about the best thing going in terms of people actually living together in the economy that Jesus taught and practiced.[2] It certainly changed my life. I am part of a community where we try—and try again when we fail—to share our money and our property, open rooms to folks who are homeless, and welcome the stranger as Christ.

But my experience of failure is exactly where I've learned that I can only receive God's economy as a gift, because the whole experiment falls apart when it's just another religious *ought*. I resent our guests. I get annoyed by people I know well. I tell God it would be a lot easier for me to believe in his love if he'd send some more lovable people. No matter how radical our "commitments," God's economy can't happen if we turn it into a religious duty.

Every time I can remember wanting to walk away from community, it's been because I thought I was carrying too much of the load or couldn't stand the feeling that one more freeloader was taking advantage of me. At those moments, I always remember the great things I think I've invested in this community—my paycheck, my time in meetings that are way too long, my great life that I'm sure I could be living if I weren't giving myself to this. I offer up my sacrifices like some ancient pagan before a flaming pyre and beg the gods to vindicate me. It's silly, I know, but I've done it many times.

And every time, the gracious God who revealed himself in Jesus waits in silence. Somehow, by grace, I eventually remember that this whole thing we call community is a gift—that my whole life is a gift—a little glimpse God has given us into the divine economy that never ends. Somehow, I remember this is not about me. It's not even about us. And the great darkness recedes. By a light that's not our own, we find a way to go on together.

If we're going to practice Jesus' tactic of eternal investments and live in God's economy now, it won't be because we're clever enough to beat the system or brave enough to challenge it. If we turn Jesus' tactics into just another religious system, we reject them. But if we can receive them as the gift that they are, then a new economy has already come. Instead of worrying about our 401(k), we can celebrate community by investing in friendships now that will sustain us when we're old. The darkness of an economic downturn may expose the lie of money's promises. But the light of Christ reveals life abundant all around.

Trusting the Lily-Maker

" 'Consider the lilies,' is the only commandment I ever obeyed," wrote Emily Dickinson.[3] We religious types could learn a lot from her honesty. If you have eyes to see, Jesus says after exposing money's conspiracy to blind us, abundant life is brimming over in the fields all around. "Look at the birds of the air; they do not sow or reap or store away in barns, and yet your heavenly Father feeds them.... See how the lilies of the field grow. They do not labor or spin. Yet I tell you that not even Solomon in all his splendor was dressed like one of these" (Matthew 6:26, 28–29). If our Father provides so extravagantly for flowers, why do we worry that he won't take care of us?

Eternal Investments:
How God's Children Plan Ahead

Well, we're prone to say in our defense, birds don't have to worry about sending their kids to college, and while lilies might look nice, they don't get a water bill from the city every month. "Consider the lilies" may be law enough for a poet, but it hardly cuts it for small-business owners and day laborers. Most of us have real lives to worry about, not to mention the starving children in Africa who don't even have enough to eat like birds. Where's God's abundance when we really need it, anyway? If our Father in heaven cares so much, why doesn't he see to the basic necessities of his children here below?

These are fair questions, especially when you're the person who is suffering. The psalmists ask these questions of God all the time. But in the midst of unanswered questions and the uncertainties of life, Jesus asks a different question: Who are you going to trust—God or money? Whether the perceived need is your family's security after you die or food security for the billion people living in extreme poverty, you have to trust *someone*. Our religious impulse says we can take care of it ourselves, thank you very much; the gospel says God has already taken care of it.

Jesus' tactic of eternal investments serves to clarify, then, a fundamental point of confusion. The question is *not* whether (a) God is able to take care of things or (b) we need to step in and fill the gap. We can never know enough to answer that kind of question with absolute certainty. But Jesus helps us see that certainty is not what we need to enter into God's economy. The *real* question is whether we trust ourselves or the God of abundance. "I want you to be part of my answer," Jesus says. "Check out the lilies. They're just a glimpse of what is possible in God's economy. Don't you want to be part of this?" God leaves us free to choose, of course. But Jesus goes out of his way to make plain the choice that is before us.

For my friend Jim, the either/or of this choice came clear when he got the life insurance policy in the mail from his dad. Starting out as an adult in the "real world," he had to decide whether he was going to make a monthly investment in the sort of security that this world offers. His decision to return the policy offended his father (it never feels good to have a gift returned). But what's much more interesting is the way his decision rubs against our sensibilities. A story like his somehow offends us, even though we weren't the ones who gave the gift. Why does it seem so wrong—so irresponsible, even—to reject our world's conventional way of planning ahead?

Trying to make sense of this, I came across an article called "God Loves Savers." The author, Paul Zane Pilzer (who, for the record, wrote a bestselling book called *God Wants You to Be Rich*), tells the story of how his immigrant father sacrificed each month to make deposits to the custodian savings account that paid for his education and helped make him the millionaire that he is today. Pilzer's father could have spent that money on himself or even on his son's more immediate desires, but instead he chose to invest it. "Saving money is more than a commendable habit," Pilzer, the son-turned-millionaire, writes. "It is a personal act of faith, a form of self-denial that expresses confidence in the future. A person who denies current comfort and pleasure for future happiness is demonstrating his or her belief in a destiny that can be controlled and improved."[4]

I'm grateful for Mr. Pilzer's forthrightness and the way it serves to further clarify the decision Jesus sets before us. The power of investment, as we saw earlier, is indeed that it makes it possible for us to deny ourselves now so that we can enjoy something better in the future. But Pilzer also reinforces the truth that what we choose to invest in is an "act of personal faith." When we entrust our treasure to something beyond our immediate desires, we make a statement of faith. Investing in a life insurance policy or a college fund for our kids or the 401(k) that's supposed to take care of us after our children have been educated and left us behind, we proclaim our faith in "a destiny that can be controlled and improved." In short, we trust ourselves because we're pretty sure that no one else is going to be as reliable —not even God.

At first blush we're likely to respond to someone who doesn't invest in life insurance by accusing him of selfishness and irresponsibility. He should think of someone other than himself, we say to ourselves. After all, investment is a sacrifice. And Jesus says we have to learn to deny ourselves. This is all true enough. But what if someone like my friend Jim decides that it's actually a wiser investment to send $25 a month to a poor kid half a world away than it is to send the same amount to a fancy suite on the 50th floor of an office building in New York City? That too would be a statement of faith. You might even consider it an investment in the One who said, "For I was hungry and you gave me something to eat, I was thirsty and you gave me something to drink, I was a stranger and you invited me in, I needed clothes and you clothed me, I was sick and you looked after me, I was in prison and you came to visit me" (Matthew 25:35–36).

Jesus' tactics take the power of investment and har-
ness it to build the bizarre yet beloved community of
God's new family. In the Roman world of the early
church, Christians were often called "atheists" because
they proclaimed with their lives and words a faith that
was unlike any religion their neighbors had seen before.
The Romans knew their economic and religious lives
were inseparable. To reject the power of money was, in
their eyes, to believe in no god at all.

But Christians knew better. They walked away from
money and its reign (which was crushing the life out of
many of them) because they heard and saw something
better in the way of Jesus. The book of Acts says "no
one claimed that any of his possessions was his own, but
they shared everything they had" and "there were no
needy persons among them" (4:32, 34). This led to incredible growth of the community in Jerusalem—"the
Lord added to their number daily" (Acts 2:47)—and
that community in turn sent missionaries out to spread
the good news of Jesus Christ to all the known world.

A few decades later we read that this same Jerusalem community was suffering persecution and didn't
have enough to feed themselves. But by then they had
family throughout the Roman Empire. On his visits
to churches, Paul took a collection to send back to the

brothers and sisters in Jerusalem and provide for their needs. They hadn't invested in a retirement plan, but in a new family instead. In their time of need, it turned out that they had brothers and sisters to take care of them. But they had more than that. They had a movement that was spreading like wildfire, making abundant life possible for people all around the world.

Reba Place Fellowship is a Christian community in Evanston, Illinois, that has mentored many young churches and Christian communities, including the Rutba House community where I live. In the summer of 2007, I was their guest for a fiftieth anniversary celebration commemorating God's faithfulness to a peculiar little group of Christians. In 1957 a group of young Mennonites got together in a neighborhood where they had volunteered and done service work. They committed themselves to the Sermon on the Mount and the strange economics that Jesus taught there. They said they would work jobs, pool their money, and take care of one another by God's grace. They decided not to invest in health insurance for themselves and their families, but to seek God's kingdom first and trust its abundance for everything else.

Fifty years later, they're still there. One way or another through the years, the bills have been paid. Babies have been born and children have been raised. People have lived their lives ... and they still don't have health insurance. What they have is even better: a group of people who've promised to take care of one another in sickness and in health ... preexisting conditions or not. The community has about forty members today, a few of whom have been there since the very beginning. They're a quirky and inspiring bunch of people. But the incredible thing about their fiftieth anniversary was that over six hundred people showed up to celebrate their life together. For three days they told stories about how this little community had changed their lives, helped their church heal, inspired beautiful witness, and supported brothers and sisters from inner-city Chicago to rural El Salvador. Their very existence is a testimony to the economics of providence. But to the people who have known them, it's more than that. It's a little taste of what God wants to give us—a life we can invest ourselves in now and enjoy for all eternity.

Jesus doesn't promise that eternal life will be easy, especially in this "time between the times" when the principalities and powers are still allowed to rebel against the Father and his children. The folks at Reba will tell you the same: even abundant life in God's economy includes sufferings. But we ought not fool ourselves.

All life in this world includes suffering. The best insurance or savings account in the world can't prevent every tragedy. Even if you could invest enough in the New York Stock Exchange to say that you owned the whole thing, your daughter could get hooked on cocaine or you could drop dead from a heart attack tomorrow. Even your investments aren't ultimately secure. The whole market could crash, after all.

The good news is this: Jesus has invited us to participate now in God's system of never-ending gift-exchange. His tactic of eternal investments shows us how we can entrust the real treasures of our lives to the Giver of all good things. To trust God in this way, though, is to entrust ourselves to the new family that God is drawing together here on earth. Our eternal investments draw us into new relationships and open our eyes to the possibility of economic friendship.

CHAPTER 6

Economic Friendship:
How Real Security Happens

TACTIC #3: *"I tell you, use worldly wealth to gain friends for yourselves."*
Luke 16:9

I grew up with people who could tell a Bible story like they'd stood there with Peter and Paul. We had preachers who could make you feel the hunger of a prodigal son chewing corn husks in a pig pen. My people know a good story when we hear it, and we always knew the Bible was full of good ones. But I'll never forget when I started to read the Bible as a teenager and realized that there are some stories in there that no one had ever told me. Jesus' story about the shrewd manager is one of them.

It's a story straight from the household economy of the ancient world, and it's set in what must have been a mighty nice enterprise. When we get some numbers toward the end of the story, some folks who keep an account with this large household owe as much as seven or eight years' wages.[1] To translate that into our contemporary setting, we're talking about a wholesale supplier that has outstanding invoices in the six-figure range. This is no small operation—it was almost certainly the biggest business in town.

At the head of this household, like a modern-day CEO, there is a rich man—a *pater familias* supreme. Everyone in town knows him, like people in Seattle know the name Bill Gates. No doubt he makes frequent trips to Jerusalem to hobnob with fellow elites and negotiate important business deals. He is invested in political negotiations and busy with self-promotion. So he needs someone he can trust to stay home and keep things running. Like every great household head in the ancient world, he needs a good manager.

This job of manager was a good one for someone who wasn't born into the elite class. It took some work to achieve—he had to be literate enough in the language of commerce to deal with basic contracts and handy enough with numbers to keep the books. A full range of people skills, product knowledge, and organizational aptitude were a must. But he also had to know his place. The *pater familias* usually didn't mind if his manager took a cut from the customers, but he didn't want him to incite the masses to revolt. More than anything, he wanted the manager to keep things going and turn a profit for the business. While the position came with privileges, it was also precarious. Managers had to be careful.

The story Jesus tells is about a manager who isn't careful enough. The head honcho happens to be in town and has either checked the bottom line or heard rumors from his customers. Maybe he's just paranoid, but he accuses his manager of "wasting his possessions" (Luke 16:1). He calls the manager in and tells him he wants an accounting. Evidently, he gives him some time to get the books together. But the manager knows he's in trouble. "My master is taking away my job," he says to himself. "I'm not strong enough to dig, and I'm ashamed to beg" (16:3). If he falls back into the lower ranks of the peasants after all these years as a manager, he'll be eaten alive. This fellow has to think fast.

So he decides to call in his master's debtors for private meetings. When they come, he asks each one how much they owe. Then he gives them a reduced bill—in one case, as much as fifty percent off! His tactic is unilateral debt reduction. He reasons this is the best way to guarantee his future security, saying to himself, "when I lose my job here, people will welcome me into their houses" (16:4). Making the best of what little time he has left in his position, the manager tries to ingratiate himself with some of his master's biggest clients.

Whether he planned it this way or not, the manager proves that he still has his wits about him, even when the pressure is on. The last thing we read in the story is that "the master commended the dishonest manager ..." (16:8). It's not exactly what you would expect from someone who's just been duped by the employee he was about to fire. The boss praises his dishonest manager. Of course, Jesus likes to tell stories with unexpected twists, so we shouldn't be too surprised. But judging from the fact that this story never came up in my Sunday school class at a good Bible-believing church, it seems to me we're not just surprised but maybe even a little *offended* by a story in which a mid-level manager trying to watch his back gets praised by his boss for shady financial dealings. What moral could a story like that possibly teach our kids?

The lesson of the story may be hidden in the tactical imagination of Jesus that we've been trying to get our heads around. If we think we have some control over the economic system we live in and are called to be upstanding and responsible stewards of wealth within it, the story of a crafty hustler like this fellow can only offend our moral sensibilities. But if we know a truer economy that has already broken into this world and doesn't have a stake in this world's rotten system, then maybe there's something to learn from this manager's instinct to use what he has to make friends. Maybe Jesus tells a story that offends our sensibilities so we can learn how economic friendship makes a new kind of security possible.

Wisdom of the Weak

I have a neighbor who has a little maxim he uses to explain much of what he sees on the news or reads about in the local paper. "Rich folks are stupid," he says to me when a millionaire files for bankruptcy or a politician gets caught embezzling money. That pretty much explains things for my neighbor. He usually doesn't say much more. If power corrupts, he figures, then money makes people stupid.

Of course, he doesn't talk that way to rich folks. He's good at knowing when to smile and when to compliment someone in power. He has made his living in service jobs. But working at restaurants and fancy hotels has only given him more evidence for his main conviction about money. Rich people are stupid because they can't begin to make a dollar go as far as his single mother, who raised five kids doing domestic work, could. What's more, rich folks think a waiter is their friend when he says, "Yes, Sir" and "Sure is a nice day, ain't it?"

Anthropologist James C. Scott says that there's a difference between the way poor people talk "onstage" and "offstage." Studying forms of everyday resistance among peasants in a small Malaysian village, he noticed how the poor and weak were good at acting like they recognized the authority of the ruling elite in public. "Onstage" they almost always gave the impression of complying with a social order in which they suffered injustice. "Offstage," however, when no one in authority was around, peasants mocked the system through gossip, slander, stealing, dragging their feet and sabotaging their masters' plans. "It is my guess," Scott writes, "that just such kinds of resistance are often the most significant and the most effective over the long run.... Everyday forms of resistance make no headlines. But just as millions of anthozoan polyps create, willy-nilly, a coral reef, so do the multiple acts of peasant insubordination and evasion create political and economic barrier reefs of their own."[2] The wisdom of the weak is that quiet tactics have a bigger impact in the long term, especially when the goal is to carve out space for a new economy within the shell of the old.

If you want to learn how to practice God's economy, you'd do better to hang out with the financial tricksters you might find in a federal prison than with the big shots who teach courses in MBA programs. At least, that seems to be the assumption of Jesus' story. The manager who wants to save his own hide doesn't try to imitate the posturing and power plays of his esteemed boss. Onstage, in the rich man's presence, he's silently compliant. But offstage, when he gets together with his master's debtors one-on-one, he pulls the sort of trick that Scott says peasants are good at.

"How much do you owe my master?" he asks the first fellow who comes in. "Eight hundred gallons of olive oil," the guy says. You can almost see the manager wink as he delivers his next line: "Take your bill, sit down quickly, and make it four hundred" (16:5–6). Alongside folks who are up to their necks in debt, this shrewd manager conspires to stick it to the Man.

To see the brilliance in this act of resistance, we

have to imagine the scene in town the next day. On the street, Simon runs into his buddy Barach and says, "Hey, listen, you're not going to believe this. Jacob over at the Big House called me in yesterday. I don't know what's got into the old boy, but he took my tab and cut it in half." Barach turns to Simon and says, "Wouldn't you know, he did the same thing for me! Not sure how long he'll keep his job if he keeps this up."

Throughout the day these fellows hear one story after another about how the manager they've been haggling with for years has suddenly turned over a new leaf and is forgiving debts owed to his master. It may well have been that the rumors and backbiting these guys engaged in offstage are exactly what got the manager in trouble with his master to start with. Then, as now, big money had ears everywhere. Nevertheless, the debtors around town start to realize what the manager has done. He's taken a big risk, and they've all benefited from it. Now it's time to get organized and look out for him.

Knowing what has happened offstage, the townsfolk go onstage to the Big House and ask to see Mr. P. Familias himself. The most articulate among them rises to give a little speech: "We want to thank you, kind sir, for your generosity," he begins. "You have always been most gracious to us, and your recent decision to reduce our debt in such a significant way is deeply appreciated. Please, sir, know that your kindness will not go unnoticed by your loyal customers." This brief statement is followed by cheers and a rousing rendition of "For He's a Jolly Good Fellow."

At any rate, the master finds himself between a rock and a hard place. On the one hand, he realizes that he's been swindled by his manager and taken a significant financial hit. No doubt, he'd strangle old Jacob if he could. But he can hardly do that because his manager has just made him town hero for the day, and any attempt to call the whole show off would only lead to an uprising. The first law of business, this rich man knows, is that you have to keep the peace. So he takes a deep breath and praises the man he was about to fire.

"The master commended the dishonest manager because he had acted shrewdly," Jesus says in the punch line to his story. Then to drive the point home, Jesus adds a little commentary about the wisdom of the weak: "For the people of this world are more shrewd in dealing with their own kind than are the people of the light" (16:8).

I guess my Sunday school teachers were right to notice that this is no morality tale. Jesus doesn't hold this manager up as an example of business ethics. He says, instead, that given what this manager knows, he's a sharp tack. Within the competitive economy of this world, he uses the wisdom of the weak to win with a poor hand. Engaging in a series of subversive acts offstage, he wins the friendship of the only people who can save his skin onstage. And, sure enough, his scheme works.

Jesus wants this story to make us think. If a white-collar criminal is smart enough to pull this off, why can't the children of God? Can't we who have seen the light of a new economy engage in tactics offstage that reveal the emptiness of this world's system for all to see? Why are we so enamored with the ways and means of this world's economy? Why must we accept the assumptions of the system?

A few years ago a friend of mine who works for a Christian NGO was part of an international consultation on how the church could address extreme poverty. This fellow has lived much of his adult life in the slums of megacities and knows well the sort of tactical imagination that keeps people alive in those places. As his colleagues in this consultation discussed the best strategy for Western Christians to address poverty, my friend made a suggestion. "Wouldn't it help," he asked, "if we invited some poor people to come and think with us about how to help them?" There was silence in the room, and then one of the more experienced relief and development workers spoke. "I'm afraid that would just slow us down."

In our rush to solve problems that are indeed urgent, we often overlook the wisdom of the weak, assuming that the losers in this world's system don't have much to offer. But Jesus insists the opposite is true: if we pay attention to the weak, we can learn the tactics of everyday resistance that are ultimately effective. If we're willing to slow down and listen, the poor can often lead us into God's economy.

My friends at Jesus People USA in Chicago have seen this with the issue of food security. Feeding the hungry is a concern that lots of people share, and there are all kinds of efforts to make this happen. I remember bringing cans of food to school as a kid, competing with my fellow classmates to see who could grab the most from our parents' cupboards for the annual Thanksgiving food drive. Nonprofit organizations invest big money in fundraising campaigns for food ministries, and advocates and lobbyists try to convince corporations and governments that it's in their best interest to meet people's basic food needs.

No doubt all of this helps. But every homeless person

knows that an ungodly amount of food gets thrown away in the United States every day. Hanging out with homeless friends, folks at Jesus People USA learned "dumpster diving"—the practice of redeeming discarded food from the trash bins behind grocery stores and restaurants before it's hauled off to the landfill. Making the rounds with homeless friends who knew the dumping patterns well, they saw that there was more than enough food to feed everyone in the homeless ministries they sponsored. So they went to the businesses in town with a proposal that would have been embarrassing to refuse: donate your trash, and we'll feed the hungry in our city. Working together, they've been doing it now for years.

When we decide that the weak are not only *objects* of our charity but also *subjects* who teach us needed wisdom, it makes new relationships possible. After all, people sense when the time you spend with them is a chore. They might smile and say thank you "onstage," but you can be sure that the poor will cuss a patronizing church like a sailor as soon as the members are out of earshot. When we enjoy the time we spend with others and honestly value their wisdom, we don't gain only new knowledge. We gain something far more valuable: a friendship that wasn't possible before.

What Money's Good For

Jesus helps us see that money is a deceptive power. Just when we think we can use it, it uses us. Money corrupts our desires and demands sacrifices at its altar. But drawing on the wisdom of the weak, Jesus also teaches what money *is* good for. "I tell you, use worldly wealth to gain friends for yourselves, so that when it is gone, you will be welcomed into eternal dwellings" (Luke 16:9). Our money may be filthy lucre, but Jesus teaches us how to corrupt the corrupting power of money: when we spread the stuff around we facilitate friendships that last forever.

The tactic of eternal investments involves learning to entrust our future to God, believing in an economics of providence. The tactic of economic friendship is similar, but it emphasizes this: *God's economy comes to us as a community of friendship.* Though Jesus made it clear that miracles happen, it's not God's standard operating procedure to rain bread from heaven or provide money from a fish's mouth. Instead, God invites us into the abundance of eternal life through economic relationships with other people.

Some of us might be slow to call this friendship. Friends, we think, are people we connect with on a deep level — people who understand us and with whom we can share our most intimate thoughts. "You can't have many true friends," we sometimes say, thinking about the time investment these special relationships require. I have a few intimate relationships like this, and I'm deeply grateful for them, but I don't think these are the sort of people Jesus is talking about when he tells us to use money to make friends.

Economic friendship is a lot more like being a good neighbor. I grew up in North Carolina's tobacco country. My Daddy's momma died of lung cancer before I really got to know her, so I can't say that I was terribly sad to see tobacco begin to disappear. But I will say this: tobacco farming taught me something about economic friendship.

Priming tobacco — pulling the broad leaves off a full-grown tobacco plant — isn't easy work. But in tobacco country, come harvest time, we did it together. When it was time to prime over at Mr. Smith's place, everyone showed up at the break of dawn with their boots on, ready to work. By noontime, when the August sun was beating down through ninety-eight percent humidity, Mrs. Smith had dinner ready and the whole crowd would sit down to eat in the yard. Pinto beans and cornbread never tasted as good as they did under a shade tree on priming day. When the work was done at the Smith's place, everyone moved on to the Jones' farm or to Mr. Bowles' fields. And on we went until everyone's tobacco was in the barns. You couldn't farm tobacco in those years without your neighbors. Totally dependent on each other, we had community whether we wanted it or not.

Jesus would have loved Mrs. Smith's cornbread too. Economic friendship isn't about buying someone we want to know better a Frappuccino—we do that on our own, because we want to. When Jesus said we should use money to make friends, he meant that we can invest what we have in interdependent, people-based economies. When we do, a new kind of community begins to emerge. Joined together in common efforts, we become God's gathered family in our neighborhoods and in the world.

On this point, I think we could take a cue from my Latino neighbors. Over the past ten years, our low-income, historically black neighborhood has seen an influx of immigrants from Mexico, El Salvador, Guatemala, and Nicaragua. It's incredible to watch how people with very few resources and limited access to the social services of this country nevertheless open their homes to a brother's family or a cousin or a friend of a friend from their old hometown. Economic friendship seems to be a natural way of life.

It's true that living conditions aren't ideal when two or three families are forced to share a small house. Theirs are not idyllic communes. As soon as people can get a place of their own, they get out. But the networks of aid and mutual dependence are strong, facilitating not only survival but also thriving communities of people whose lives are bound together. You only need to overhear the sounds of parties around here on a Saturday night to know that these folks enjoy one another more than most middle-class Americans.

If common biology, language, and culture can inspire that kind of community and economic sharing, why is it that we who say we're baptized into eternal unity in Christ's body strive so hard for economic independence and send our surplus to organizations who serve the poor on our behalf? We seem to be more enamored with the security and luxury of success than with the wisdom of the weak and God's economy of abundance—if there's another explanation, I'd love to hear it. We spend more time with people who can help us get ahead than we do with the brothers and sisters God saw fit to give us. As a result, we know precious little of economic friendship. We're not very good at loving our neighbors because we don't think we need them now—and we hope we never do. No wonder we're lonely.

We need to hear the words of Paul's first letter to Timothy: "Command those who are rich in this present world not to be arrogant nor to put their hope in wealth, which is so uncertain, but to put their hope in God, who richly provides us with everything for our enjoyment." All are invited into God's abundance, even the rich. But what we do with our money is important. "Command them to do good, to be rich in good deeds, and to be generous and willing to share. In this way they will lay up treasure for themselves as a firm foundation for the coming age, so that they may take hold of the life that is truly life" (1 Timothy 6:17–19).

The idolatry of wealth doesn't only compromise our relationship with God; it destroys community and makes abundant life impossible. But if we're "generous and willing to share," we disarm the power of money and set it free to build the beloved community that God wants everyone to enjoy. When we employ the tactic of economic friendship, we can begin to enjoy—here and now—the neighbors with whom Jesus promises we will dance for all eternity. Doesn't that sound like more fun than living in luxurious isolation in a gated community?

Imagine, for example, what economic friendship could look like at your church. If your church is like most churches in America, odds are people there don't talk much about their money. Every so often the preacher gives a sermon on tithing or providing for the needy. And if you're making your budget, you probably at least have a core of people who give regularly, glad for the chance to give back to God. Other than the monthly potluck supper or Christmas gift exchange, though, most churches don't have a great deal of economic exchange among their members.

But again, if your church is anything like most, you probably have some members with what we call "surplus capital." Others in your congregation most likely carry some debt—a mortgage at six percent interest or a credit card at sixteen percent that won't be paid off for forty years. Now, imagine the conversation if people from those two groups sat down for a family business meeting to talk about money.

Some exchanges could probably be arranged among this group at no cost to anyone. If the person with extra money invested in a mutual fund with an average six percent yield agreed to cash out her investment and pay off her brother's credit card bill, she could save him an incredible amount of money in compounded interest.

If he, in turn, paid her back at the same rate that the mutual fund had been paying, she would be none the poorer for it. But they would both probably get to know one another better. Who knows what gifts they might discover that they have to share with one another?

We're not even talking about extreme generosity here—simply a decision to invest in relationships with fellow church members instead of relationships with financial institutions. But maybe that little act of faith is all we need. Maybe God's generosity has already made a whole new economy possible—if we will trust it.

If we let our imaginations wander even further into the radical abundance of God's economy, the possibilities branch into an ever-growing tree of grace and gifts. Cars are swapped. College tuitions are covered. Mortgages are saved and businesses are invested in. Winter coats and turkeys and surgeries and language classes are paid for and provided. Money flows back and forth, and every time it moves, its corrupting power is turned into the goodness of God's economic abundance. Each member of the body thinks, *If I have money, why not share it?*

If you've let me take you this far in our thought experiment, I reckon you've had to suppress a voice in your head that says something like, "It would be great if church worked that way, but what do you do when Susan doesn't pay you back or Roy moves to L.A. and isn't part of your congregation anymore?" Money is messy, after all. Do we really want our church life to be disrupted by the awkward conversations you have when you share money with people? And it's not all feel-good gifting: some people are up to their necks in debt because they're irresponsible. Others feel demeaned when they have to receive help. Some folks who have money don't want to belittle those with less. Others wish they could help, but they don't know how.

It's true: economic friendships open up a can of worms. You can hardly get involved with someone else's money without getting involved in their whole life. But isn't that what church is supposed to be about—facing the truth about who we really are and loving one another because Christ already loves us? "Brothers [and sisters], if someone is caught in a sin," Paul says, "you who are spiritual should restore him gently" (Galatians 6:1). We don't get high and mighty about other people's debts and trespasses. We pray, "Forgive us our debts, as we forgive our debtors." We're all sinners, and long before each of us ran up a sin tab we could never pay, Jesus died and rose to set things right. So Paul exhorts us, "Carry each other's burdens, and in this way you will fulfill the law of Christ" (6:2).

Besides, if we signed up for fairness, we chose the wrong religion. Economic friendship is about subverting the power of money by sharing our wealth as Jesus shares his very life. If it's good for nothing else, money is good for this: it gives us a chance to show the world what grace looks like by sharing it freely in the economy of Christ's abundance.

Faithfulness in Small Things

But is it really enough for small communities of people to share their money? Given the systemic economic injustice we're up against in this world, don't we need something more than economic friendship? It's hard to imagine how talking to folks at your church about money could make a difference for the forty million people in the United States who don't have health insurance or the billion people around the world who live on less than a dollar a day.

A January 2008 study conducted by United for a Fair Economy estimated that the subprime mortgage crisis we were experiencing at that time would ultimately result in a net loss of \$164–213 billion in assets for people of color.[3] A friend pointed out to me that this was, in market terms, almost certainly the largest transfer of wealth away from black people in a very long history of economic injustice. By all accounts, the subprime crisis was the result of bad lending policies by banks who wanted to capitalize on a lucrative securities market.

If our churches had been ready to extend economic friendship to brothers and sisters who lost their homes to foreclosure, that would have been a powerful good. Truth told, Christians in the United States almost certainly had access to enough resources that we could have kept each of our brothers and sisters caught up in the subprime crisis from losing their homes. But surely such wide-reaching economic challenges demand more than the uncoordinated efforts of individuals and small groups. Doesn't God's economy offer an organized alternative to the systemic economic troubles we face?

As banks reported huge losses and markets took a dive in the winter of 2008, I was struck by an article titled "Islamic Banks Shielded from Subprime."[4] At that point, the author said, conventional global banks like CitiGroup and UBS had already written down more than \$80 billion in losses. Islamic banks, however, reported almost no loss at all. Because *sharia* law (like the Bible) forbids usury, Islamic banks do not charge interest or trade debt. "Many of these conventional products that have been under stress lately are very complex and need special risk-management tools," explained Rasheed al-Maraj, the governor of Bahrain's central bank. "In Islamic banking you will not have this kind of thing. Some of these products would not be *sharia* accepted."

This got me interested in Islamic banking, so I did a little research. It turns out that Muslims have a long history of just the sort of economic friendship that I've witnessed among my Latino neighbors. When members of the community need money for a large purchase, they typically borrow it from fellow Muslims. But Islamic law's ban on *riba*—or interest—has forced the Muslim community to think differently about money lending. If you can't make money on money, banking isn't the big business we often imagine it to be in the West. "We are not run-of-the-mill marketing people who find a niche and run with it," says Yahia Abdul-Rahman, the CEO of Lariba, an Islamic bank based in Pasadena, California. "We are humble servants of the community."[5]

What if Christians in this country took the law of

Christ as seriously as Muslim banks seem to take their law? Economic friendship is an invitation to begin living God's economy with the people closest to us. Because it is a tactic, no act of sharing is too small. Any of us can do it, even if all we have to offer is the truth about our debt. A tactical imagination teaches us to be faithful in small things — to know the truth both about our brokenness and about God's grace in relationship with fellow members of God's family. Nothing prevents these small acts of faithfulness from growing into bigger partnerships. The key, Jesus seems to say, is that we begin with small things. "Whoever can be trusted with very little can also be trusted with much" (Luke 16:10).

About twenty-five years ago, the pastor of a relatively poor congregation had an accident and racked up a huge medical bill in the hospital. Without health insurance, he lay in bed praying about how his family would survive the mounting debt. Meanwhile, his church got together, negotiated the bill with the hospital, and pooled money from its members to pay off the bill. The pastor was so overjoyed with relief that he said, "If you can do this for me, we ought to be able to do this for anyone of us who isn't insured." So that church started a little health care co-op. They didn't have a whole lot of money, but they wanted to be faithful to one another and use what they had to make sure no one was crushed by medical bills.[6]

When my family joined this same co-op a few years ago, there were over 25,000 members. Every month we get a newsletter that tells us how millions of dollars are being shared around the country to meet the needs of brothers and sisters who are sick with cancer or having babies or recovering from a car wreck. There's no way we can befriend all these people, but our common conviction that we should bear one another's burdens as members of the body of Christ has made economic friendship possible through this health care co-op. Because tens of thousands of people have committed to be faithful in little ways, a real alternative to health insurance is available for a family like mine.

This real alternative was not the result of a grand strategy to reform our nation's broken health care system. It was the fruit of a tactical imagination that started with a pastor praying in his hospital bed and some regular church folks talking about how they could share their money. Economic friendship like this may be the best witness we have to offer our neighbors in a country where over forty million people are uninsured. Americans have heard a lot of ideas in recent years about how to reform our health care system. In the meantime, though, people are hungry for some good news when their kids get sick or their parents are dying. The wisdom of Jesus' body is as practical as it is surprising.

Our preferential option for the wisdom of the weak doesn't excuse us from addressing the systemic injustices that exist in our world today. Anyone who spends time with the poor knows that governmental policy and corporate practices have a huge impact on the daily lives of folks who struggle to make ends meet. We cannot sit back in silence when the poor and weak are crushed by these powers. The argument for Jesus' subversive tactics isn't a prohibition against engaging broader societal evils.

But when we engage in the tactic of economic friendship, we are not primarily fighting for the sake of poor people we don't know. We're receiving the gift of friendship with poor and rich brothers and sisters in God's economy. Sharing our money with one another, we join the beloved community that every creature was made to delight in. Perhaps we learn the faith that this economy of abundance requires through thousands of small choices, but that hardly makes it a little thing. To be faithful in the smallest act of economic friendship is to step into the biggest possible economic alternative — God's never-ending abundance that is offered to all.

CHAPTER 7

Relational Generosity:
How We Share
Good News

TACTIC #4: *"Give to*
the one who asks you."
Matthew 5:42

Whatever road we end up walking, none of us walks alone. Long before we could walk at all, someone carried us, held us by the hand, and picked us up when we fell down. Jesus' tactic of economic friendship makes this much clear: "Christ is present to us insofar as we are present to each other."[1] Abundant life is a life we enjoy together with the family God. The early church summed it up by saying, "Outside the church there is no salvation."

The first three tactics we've looked at help us

understand why this material life with our spiritual family is vital. Without the beloved community that takes shape when we practice subversive service, eternal investment, and economic friendship, *we have no good news in the concrete here and now.* Life together, lived in God's radical abundance, is truly good news worth sharing.

This doesn't mean that the people who follow Jesus are perfect. As St. Augustine said, the church is a community of believers "on the way" to the city of God. How we live points to what we will be, but we're not there yet. We mess up together just like we mess up on our own. But a beloved community where we enjoy one another without interruption is where we're headed. Jesus' first three tactics for a good life now root us in this vision of eternal life together with God's people.

Eternal life is available now for anyone who trusts the peculiar way to God that Jesus shows us. But there is more to the way of Jesus than the way we live with fellow church members. Jesus' tactical imagination also insists we think about how our community engages the world around us. This is important not only because God loves the world, but because Jesus knows that children of his Father need the "outsider." It wasn't fellowship at my local church that first opened my eyes to

God's radical abundance; it was, instead, a homeless guy crouched over a Styrofoam cup outside Union Station.

I was saved by someone who didn't fit my idea of "God's people." Maybe he was born with a mental disability into a family that was too poor to take care of him. Maybe he fought in Vietnam and never could shake the nightmares. Maybe he took a hit of crack cocaine early in life and became a slave to the power of addiction. I don't know. But I do know God used that fellow to save me. I know I needed him to help me see God's abundance more fully.

We can't read the more than two thousand verses in Scripture that refer to the poor without recognizing that the gospel isn't good news until it's good news for the poor. This may be the biggest shift in evangelical missions over the past twenty years. From Rick Warren to Franklin Graham, the most prominent evangelical leaders of this generation have made an unequivocal commitment to evangelism *and* social action. People who are starving and dressed in rags don't want to hear someone read a list of propositional "good news." They want to *see* the good news in action. The church doesn't hold revival meetings and call it a day — we feed the hungry, clothe the naked, dig wells, and staff medical clinics. Social action isn't an optional part of evangelism; it *is* evangelism.

This is an important correction to the overspirituality that dominated evangelical Christianity just a generation ago. But the both/and of holistic mission still misses the heart of Jesus if we don't see that *the church needs the poor as much as the poor need the church*. Jesus didn't embrace the poor only because he pitied them or because he knew he had the resources to help them. Jesus embraced the poor because they were rushing into the kingdom ahead of the scribes and Pharisees—those who called themselves God's people. Jesus welcomed people who knew poverty because they were ready to receive what he had to offer. Religious people, he said, could learn something from them.

Our spiritual lives are linked to the material conditions of our life. When we feel like we don't need much materially, we often have trouble remembering why we need God. We comfortable Americans can go through an entire day without thinking of God. But Jesus gave the poor more than food to eat and relief from their sickness. He restored them to God's beloved community. "The sick are not just healed," Albert Borgmann writes of the crowds who came to Jesus; "their sins are forgiven; they are freed of hostility and despair, i.e., of their helpless efforts to master their deficiency."[2] Because the poor know their ultimate neediness, they are ready to receive the gift of new life that never ends.

God does not take pleasure in the suffering of poor people. God is as grateful as we are that advances like antibiotics and good public water treatment have drastically reduced infant mortality and other manifestations of extreme poverty since the time of Jesus. But beggars force us to confront the truth that we cannot solve all of our problems—and that our solutions create still more problems. We cannot save ourselves any more than the pre-teen sex slave in India can save herself. We need to be saved. We need a Savior.

Along with his plan to build a beloved community of wholeness in the midst of a broken world, Jesus also gives us tactical advice about how to engage our neighbors—especially the poor. Relational generosity may be the most evangelistic tactic of Jesus' economic vision. "Give to the one who asks you," Jesus says, "and do not turn away from the one who wants to borrow from you" (Matthew 5:42). In a world where the poor are often cast as our enemies, Jesus invites us into revelatory relationships. Sharing with the poor, he says, we receive the gift of friendship. In return, our friends who are poor provide us the eyes we need to see the truth about our world.

Love Casts Out Fear

Jesus introduces his tactic of relational generosity in the Sermon on the Mount. It's the last in a series of tactics he offers as an extension of the law that said, "Eye for eye, and tooth for tooth" (Matthew 5:38; Exodus 21:24; Leviticus 24:20; Deuteronomy 19:21). Because we usually think of ourselves when we think about laws, we're prone to read "an eye for an eye" as justification for the retribution we want when someone else violates our rights. Matthew 5:38 is probably the most quoted verse in support of the death penalty, for example. If someone takes a life—especially when it's a brutal murder—something in many of us says they deserve to die. Eye for eye, life for life.

While that may fit our notions of justice, Jesus suggests that *retribution* isn't the intent of God's law. "Eye for eye" is, instead, a *limit* on retributive violence in a world where people find it easy to justify killing. If you poked a guy's eye out in the ancient Near East, his brothers might get together and try to kill you. In that context, "eye for eye, and tooth for tooth" was a measure of restraint. You can't take any more than what is taken from you, God said.

In his Sermon on the Mount, Jesus says he has come to "fulfill" God's law (Matthew 5:17). Knowing the spirit of the law from its beginning, Jesus extends its core teachings to their ultimate goal. He reveals what he and the Father always had in mind. "You have heard that it was said, 'Eye for eye, and tooth for tooth,' but I tell you, Do not resist an evil person" (5:38–39). People who have been adopted into our Father's household don't need to settle the score when others do us wrong. We don't answer hate with hate. Instead, we overcome evil with good.

To people in power, a tactic like this sounds strange. But for people who have suffered under oppressive and racist regimes, this law is good news. Gandhi, who was not himself a Christian but read the Sermon on the Mount every morning, used this insight as the basis for his nonviolent campaign to end the British occupation of India. Dr. Martin Luther King Jr. preached it time and again in the American South, even when white people spit in the faces of black children and sprayed them with fire hoses. King chose to love his enemies even when he saw they were going to kill him. Darkness cannot drive out darkness, he insisted. Only light can — and it doesn't matter how small the light. If it keeps on shining, it can illuminate the darkest night.

The genius of nonresistance is in its ability to expose the lies we tell ourselves, the lies of the powers and principalities — especially the lies that become institutionalized in society. The great lie of the Jim Crow South was that people with black skin are inherently inferior to people with white skin. This wasn't just a belief in some people's head. It was the assumption of everyday social institutions. Forty years later, "Whites only" signs seem foreign to us, but they were as normal as stop signs in the living memory of most of my neighbors over the age of fifty.

Like the nonresistance of the civil rights movement, relational generosity unveils a lie that is hidden in plain sight. By giving to the one who asks, we welcome the stranger as someone who might become a friend. We interrupt our society's normal way of seeing the poor. Though we rarely say it out loud, the assumption of our social institutions and daily interactions is that beggars are outsiders to be feared. Jesus teaches us a tactic to expose the darkness of this lie and help us imagine new ways of engaging our neighbors who happen to be in need.

When I was in college just outside of Philadelphia, I

had a professor who wanted us to become shrewd and savvy Christians who could critically engage the culture around us. He taught us to read serious public intellectuals and took us to art museums and cultural events, exposing us to the best that one of this country's great cities had to offer. I'll never forget the night he took us to hear the symphony in Center City, Philadelphia. We were walking home after meeting the conductor and pianist backstage when a homeless fellow asked if any of us could spare some change. He walked with us for a couple of blocks, and one of my classmates handed him a few quarters.

At the next intersection, our professor turned to face us on the sidewalk. He raised a finger in the air to punctuate the point he was about to make. Then he declared with great passion, "Never, never, never give money to a panhandler!" He spun around on his heal abruptly and continued to the van without another word. I guess he thought he'd said all he needed to say.

People offer lots of reasons not to give money to beggars on the street. Some say it enables destructive habits like addiction, only hurting the person who is asking for help. Others say you can't give to everyone who asks, so you might as well give what you can to organizations that provide shelter, food, and services to the homeless. Some people say dropping a dollar in a beggar's cup may ease your conscience, but it only reinforces a dehumanizing system of dependence. There is some truth in all of these explanations, but none of them explain to me the vehemence with which my professor declared an absolute prohibition on giving to someone who asks. None of these reasoned arguments names the source of the knot I still feel in my stomach when I see someone on the street who I think might ask me for money.

In both Matthew and Luke's gospels, Jesus presents the tactic of relational generosity as part of his teaching on loving our enemies (Matthew 5:39; Luke 6:27). Our problem with beggars, Jesus seems to say, is that we imagine them to be our enemies. Most of us would rather not think too deeply about people who are poor that way. We want to think that we pity them or perhaps that we'd like to help them. But the last thing we want to do is consider that their poverty has anything to do with us.

Those of us who have access to resources don't like to name the poor as our enemies. But our fear of beggars and our efforts to control people who happen to be poor reveal the dividing lines that the poor already see so clearly. Through nonresistance, Jesus' tactic of relational generosity exposes our fear of the poor. By giving to the one who asks, we don't deny our fear. Instead, we act in faith that love can drive out fear. When it does, friendship becomes possible where there was only division before. And friendship across the dividing lines of our world may be just what we need to really know the abundance of the life that we were made for.

Interruptive Friendships

When I was getting to know homeless folks on the streets of Philadelphia, I became friends with a guy named Anthony. Anthony's buddies called him "Wilderness Man," and he was proud of his ability to brave the harsh Northeastern winters with some good hiking boots and the contents of a single backpack. Anthony had been homeless a long time. He knew how to survive.

As I got to know Anthony, he slowly dropped his tough-man front and told me his story. Abandoned by all the people who might have loved him, he'd been on the streets since he was a kid. He started traveling with other homeless men to stay safe and have some sense of belonging. Some of those guys introduced him to crack as a way to escape from his troubles, and he got hooked.

For the past few years he had watched it weaken his strong, young body. Anthony said he wanted to get clean, and he asked if I could help him.

So I went to the best recovery program I knew in Philadelphia and asked the director if she could make room for Anthony. She said she would, and I drove Anthony to check him into the residential program a few days later. During his "blackout" when Anthony couldn't contact anyone from his former life, I called the program director to see how he was doing. She was hopeful, saying that he seemed to be determined. When I called her a few days later, though, she told me Anthony had checked himself out. He said he couldn't stand it anymore—he was going back to the streets.

I saw Anthony a few weeks later, back on the same boulevard where I'd met him a couple of years before. He was hesitant to speak, ashamed of what he assumed was his own failure. "I just couldn't do it," he told me, looking down at his feet. After a pause, he looked up. "But I'm the Wilderness Man, you know. I'll be all right out here."

That's the last time I saw Anthony. But his honesty in the time I knew him invited me into his world. Anthony bore some responsibility for the decisions he'd made, but I also knew that his world was the underside of an economy we shared. Homelessness wasn't just Anthony's problem. It was my problem too. How could I call Anthony my friend and watch him walk back into a life that we both knew would kill him? Befriending Anthony made me ask how my own life needed to change.

My race to the White House was interrupted by a nameless fellow outside Union Station, but friends like Anthony forced me to rethink my assumptions about helping the poor. I had assumed that addiction was a personal problem to be fixed—a sickness that could be cured, like the occasional ear infection I treat with antibiotic drops. Serving the poor, I figured, was about using the resources I've been blessed with to meet their needs. The church has soup lines to feed the hungry. Christians have benevolence funds to help the needy. We take addicts to treatment programs and pray that they'll get well. When they don't … well, at least we did our part. They must not have really wanted to change.

But Anthony was my friend. I knew he wanted to be free from addiction. And I was beginning to see how his addiction was tied up with the sickness of a society that was so afraid of him that he had never really been loved. My friendship with Anthony helped me see how some of our social services and ministries to the poor are unintentionally designed to manage the poor's problems while maintaining the wall between "them" and "us." Homeless shelters don't end homelessness because they never question the assumptions and lifestyles of those of us who aren't homeless. They can't afford to — our donations keep them in business.

The only answer to homelessness, Anthony helped me to see, is homes where broken people are welcomed as children of God. God used a difficult friendship with Anthony to help me find my way to the hospitality house where I live today. At the Rutba House community, we are committed to making space for friendship with people who are poor and homeless. Because we believe Jesus may show up in the disguise of a beggar, we keep a "Christ room" in our homes for people who have nowhere else to live. If someone on the street asks us for money to buy some food, we invite them home to our table for dinner. When I was solicited by a prostitute a few years ago, driving home late one night, I asked her why she felt like she needed to sell herself to a random guy on the street. She told me she was hungry, so I invited her to come home for a meal. My wife sat at our kitchen table and got to know her while I cooked a grilled cheese sandwich.

I don't know that relational generosity is any more

effective at fixing people's problems than strategic plans to end poverty by 2020. I'm definitely not saying that we shouldn't sign on to the UN's development goals or the One Campaign. Evil and oppressive structures need to change. But we have to change as well. Our imaginations need to be renewed. Whatever our political persuasion, we're always tempted to blame our political enemies for the troubles in the world and think that real change will happen when the policies we endorse are put into practice. But whatever good we might effect on a national or global scale, we can be sure that it will come with unintended negative consequences.

Not so with relational generosity, however. Jesus doesn't teach us to practice relational generosity because it will "fix" the poor. He invites us to give to whoever asks so we might be children of our Father in heaven. Yes, God's love transforms lives. We know this from our own experience and from the testimony of others. But God doesn't ask *us* to change people — God asks us to *love* people. When we share with one who asks, we are changed. Little by little, we grow into the love of our Father, whose love is perfect.

This is not easy, and I don't want to idealize it. As broken and needy people, it's hard to love other people who are broken and needy too. A couple of years ago, a woman in our community was pregnant. To ease the pain in her back, she was taking daily walks in the neighborhood. One day when she was out walking, a fellow named Larry asked her for some money. She didn't know Larry, but she told him if he wanted to walk home with her, our community would do what we could to help him. So Larry made his way to Rutba House.

I admit, I was suspicious of Larry from the start. He was a fast talker who claimed to be a preacher as soon as he learned that we were Christians. I doubted he wanted anything more than his next high. But others at the house gave him the benefit of the doubt. When he said his washing machine had broken, someone offered to do his laundry. Pretty soon Larry was coming by once a day to get his clean clothes. He often demanded something to eat and became frustrated if his clothes weren't ready.

Jesus said we should give to everyone who asks, but I'm pretty sure Jesus didn't mean that we should give to everyone *whatever* they ask. If our generosity really is relational, it seems to me that there comes a time in a relationship when you have to be honest about how you feel. So one day when Larry was yelling about something he needed, I told him I didn't like the way he used us. Larry, in turn, told me that he knew from the first time he laid eyes on me that I had Satan on the inside. I said, "You care more about getting a fix than you do about me — or yourself." He said, with a fist raised in front of his face, "I ought to lay you out."

That's when I decided to sit down. Larry was mad, and I was getting mad too. I had been sitting on my suspicions about Larry, and it looked like I'd been right. But even if I was right, it didn't help anything. Jesus asked me to love Larry. Nothing I say is going to fix him. But God can transform Larry. And God can heal me as I learn to walk patiently with Larry in his addiction.

"Need alone is the poor man's worthiness," wrote St. John Chrysostom, the great fourth-century preacher from Constantinople. "We show mercy on him not because of his virtue but because of his misfortune, in order that we ourselves may receive from the Master his great mercy."[3] It's not our job to figure out who the deserving poor are. Relational generosity isn't a tactic we master so we can feel good about knowing when to give and when not to. Instead, Jesus invites us into the brokenness of real relationships where we can know our own neediness alongside the poor. It's a messy business, but Jesus says this is how we grow in love, learning over and over again just how much our Father loves us.

Uncalculated Giving

One thing I've learned living among people who've survived poverty is that they're not very impressed by charity. They'll accept it, sure — but they're not impressed. Social clubs give awards to philanthropists. Newspapers honor benevolence. But the poor suspect that most giving from the well-to-do is little more than guilt therapy and image management. St. Vincent de Paul, who gave his life in service to the poor, said, "It is only for your love alone that the poor will forgive you the bread you give to them."[4]

Not long ago I was sitting on the porch with my neighbor, reading our local paper and talking about the news. In the "Metro" section that day, there happened to be an article about a volunteer group that had helped clean up some yards in our neighborhood. "Have you ever noticed," my neighbor said to me, "that every time those folks come over here they bring a camera?" He'd noticed. And he wasn't impressed.

Immediately after Jesus says that relational generosity is meant to grow us up into the love of our Father, so that we can be perfect—or complete—as our Father's love is complete, he gives us a warning: "Be careful not to do your 'acts of righteousness' before men, to be seen by them. If you do, you will have no reward from your Father" (Matthew 6:1). Jesus also noticed that people who are given access to the abundance of God's creation have the incredible ability to believe that it makes them important. Because we're impressed by wealth, we're also impressed by people who have enough to be magnanimous—to make a name for themselves with their giving.

But like my neighbor, Jesus is not impressed. He says we're missing the point if our generosity shines the light on us, highlighting the division between the haves and the have-nots, the giver and the receiver. The point of sharing, after all, is that God's light from above has revealed the lie of economic division. If we try to step into the limelight, we've forfeited the very abundance that our Father was trying to shower on us.

The antidote to this spiritual sickness, Jesus says, is that we give "in secret" (Matthew 6:4). We don't hold press conferences to announce our generosity. We give to the one who asks. Because we treasure our relationships with others above all else, we do everything we can not to highlight their need or diminish their dignity. Our giving is not the big deal. The big deal is our relationship with one another and the communion with our Father that grows deeper as we're reconciled with people we used to think of as enemies. The big deal is how our sharing with others helps us become God's beloved community.

Of course, Jesus says early in the Sermon on the Mount that this community he is gathering us into will shine like a city on a hill (Matthew 5:14–16). To give in secret is not to give "privately," building up our egos through the false humility of anonymous gifts. How could our generosity be relational if we never come face-to-face with people who are in need? To give in secret is, instead, to give without concern for our image or for results. It is to give like our Father, who "sends rain on the righteous and the unrighteous" (5:45).

Jesus' tactic of relational generosity challenges our notions of "good stewardship." Most of us with money think our decisions about its use are very important. In all earnestness, we imagine ourselves as the stewards of a household where the head honcho is absent but could come at any time and ask for a reckoning. We want to look good when the boss is looking, so we are fastidious about our accounting. The Lord asks for a tithe, so we carefully calculate our ten percent. (*Some people* tithe on net income, but we take pride in knowing that *we* are tithing on the gross.) Or we decide that our local church is not as good a steward as we are, so we give symbolically in worship and then carefully choose the nonprofit organizations that we want to support. We balance our global and local concerns by supporting Bread for the World and the local homeless shelter. We pray over these decisions and even give sacrificially at times. With careful calculation, we try and we try to get our giving right.

But Jesus says, "When you give to the needy, do not let your left hand know what your right hand is doing" (6:3). I love how Clarence Jordan illuminates this teaching. "When people give grudgingly or for show," he writes, "their hearts are not in their gift. They will reach into their pocket with their right hand, and then with their left hand they will carefully count out the exact amount they wish to give.... Every deed is recorded in detail, and due pride is taken therein. But when people give in secret, or 'from the heart,' they reach into their pocket with their right hand and take out all that's there and hand it over to meet the need."[5] They don't take time to calculate how their gift will be viewed by others or whether it is the most responsible use of resources. They just give to the one who asks.

They love the person in front of them and so create the possibility of a whole new relationship.

My friend Paul runs a small business in upstate New York. He's a good entrepreneur who balances the books every month and provides jobs for about forty people. But he also embodies for me this notion of uncalculated giving. I know from people who work for him that he makes about the same as everyone else at the company, whether they sit at a desk or pack boxes in the shipping department. Paul doesn't make a big deal of it, but he does tell his coworkers that they're all in the same boat. They're like an extended family. And they invite their customers into that community. They encourage them to call and catch up rather than send an order by email. They tell them to pay their invoices when they can.

Once when I was visiting Paul at his office, a guy who wanted to talk stopped by. It was pretty clear that he was homeless. Paul chatted with him, answering questions about his kids and listening to the fellow talk about his struggles. After a while Paul said he figured he better get back to work, but he invited his friend to come by and see him at home sometime. Paul told me later that the homeless man sometimes sleeps in his office at home. They've known each other for a long time; Paul trusts him.

Because executives don't make much more than laborers at Paul's company, they turn a good profit most months. Rather than reinvest their winnings in expansion, though, Paul likes to invest in people who are out of work. He has established a culture of grace and interdependence in the office, and it has become a place of healing for people who need to get back on their feet. They earn a paycheck doing real work, but they also gain a community. Relational generosity invites them into transformative friendship.

The thing that strikes me most about Paul is that he's not impressed by his own righteousness. He is, as a matter of fact, rather unimpressed. He knows the power of money, but he has his hands on money every day. So rather than try to keep them clean, he seems to play this game of not letting the left one know what the right one is doing. I imagine his bookkeeper gets a little nervous sometimes, but I suspect he's closer to the kingdom of God than a lot of people who think themselves more radical. It seems like he gets it: sharing what we have in the world is a way of both extending the beloved community God invites us into and remembering what's at its heart—the radical abundance of a Father who loves without limit and gives without calculating the cost.

CHAPTER 8

Gracious Politics:
How to Live
Under Occupation

TACTIC #5: *"Give to Caesar what is Caesar's and to God what is God's."*
Mark 12:17

M atthew, Mark, and Luke all report that Jesus ran into some trouble after the community that he was gathering grew into a mob and set up a street theater-like "triumphal procession" to welcome their King into Jerusalem (see Mark 11:1ff, Matthew 21:1ff, Luke 19:28ff). Evidently, Jesus' tactics were working. People flocked to join this new movement, even though Jesus had opted against a strategic marketing plan to broadcast his message and create a buzz. Thousands of small acts on the margins erupted into a march on

Jerusalem. What had been germinating underground broke through for all to see. By every account, the authorities were not pleased.

Mark says that the "chief priests, the teachers of the law and the elders" came to Jesus and asked what authority he thought he had to march into Jerusalem, disturbing the peace of the Temple and proclaiming a new way of life for God's people. What follows in all the synoptic accounts is a great public debate in the Temple courts. Everyone who has any authority in Jerusalem sends their smartest guys to question Jesus in front of the crowds and try to catch him in his words. Now that Jesus' movement has ignited the public, everyone wants to know what he's really about.

"Teacher," one group says to him, careful not to disrespect a popular leader in front of his supporters, "we know you are a man of integrity. You aren't swayed by men, because you pay no attention to who they are; but you teach the way of God in accordance with the truth." The language is polite, but it's a setup from the start. These people don't want to learn from Jesus. They want to trap him. So they pretend to be seekers in order to ask a question that will expose Jesus as the dangerous revolutionary they think he is. "Is it right to pay taxes to Caesar or not?" (Mark 12:14).

Their question is a litmus test, set up either to disappoint and disperse the crowd following Jesus, or to give the Roman authorities reason to arrest Jesus as a rabble-rouser. Jesus has just been welcomed into Jerusalem as a king. The religious authorities know that if he says, "Be good citizens and pay your taxes," the people will think Jesus doesn't offer any real challenge to the occupying forces of Rome. If, on the other hand, Jesus tells the people not to pay their taxes, the religious leaders won't have to worry about him anymore, since he'll be inside a Roman jail for sedition. The clever Pharisees and Herodians think they've caught Jesus in the perfect trap.

The first rule of trapping Jesus is that if you think you have, you haven't. Jesus asks them why they're trying to trick him, exposing their motive, but then before they can answer he asks them to bring him a denarius, the Roman coin that was in circulation at the time. "Whose portrait is this? And whose inscription?" Jesus asks. It was Caesar's money, so Caesar's name and face were written all over it. Everyone knew that, but Jesus made the religious authorities say it. Then he answered their question: "Give to Caesar what is Caesar's and to God what is God's."

The crowds chuckled, no doubt, because they knew their King had answered well. The Pharisees and

Herodians fell silent because they knew they hadn't been able to trap Jesus. But the followers of Jesus — those who would become his body in the world — heard in his answer an effective tactic for engagement with the political powers.

Whatever steps we take to live the abundant life that Jesus has made possible, we can't ignore the fact that we live in the midst of political systems that affect us and our neighbors. Beloved community happens here and now, but it never happens in a vacuum. God's economy intersects with the economies of this world. We pay (or don't pay) our taxes and our tithes with bills that bear the images of dead leaders and the inscriptions of nation-states. Wherever we find ourselves, God's people live under occupation in this world, negotiating the power of rulers who have not yet submitted all things to our Creator. Jesus doesn't ask us to flee from the world or take it over. Instead, he invites us to give to Caesar what is Caesar's and to God what is God's. He gives us a tactic for how to live as a people under occupation until the whole universe submits to our King.

For most of his young adult life, Pat worked sixty-hour weeks as a lawyer in western Massachusetts. He made a good living, had a nice home, and was able to give his kids most of the things they wanted. In many ways, Pat was living the American Dream. But he knew that something was wrong. Pat's wife, Debbie, told him he was drinking too much. He tried to deny that he had a problem, but Pat knew he couldn't stop drinking. Tension at home eventually escalated to the point that Pat saw he was going to have to choose between his family and the bottle—and he couldn't stand the thought of losing either.

That's when Pat met Jesus. It sounds too good to be true, but Pat had a profound conversion experience just as his life was falling apart. He discovered freedom from alcoholism and new energy to love Debbie and their kids. He had almost wrecked the good life he was failing to enjoy, but God showed up at just the last minute to save the life Pat had always wanted.

Or so it seemed. But a few years later, Pat and Debbie's pastor prophesied that they would be living in the inner city within a year. They had no plans to leave their house in the suburbs, but in the months after their pastor's prophecy, Pat and Debbie started to see how relationships with people across social and economic dividing lines were good news to them. When they sold their home in the suburbs and moved to the inner city, it felt less like a sacrifice than a chance to enjoy God's abundant life.

Pat and Debbie's story puts flesh on Jesus' tactics for a good life now. Through relational generosity, they found their way into a new lifestyle and a new family called Nehemiah House. Together with other Christians, they practice economic friendship through a relational tithe circle where members put ten percent of their incomes into a common pot and share it so that no one among them will be in need. According to the script of the American Dream, Pat and Debbie should be enjoying the well-deserved fruit of their years of hard work. Instead, they live in a sprawling old boarding house and think nothing of cooking for thirty people and then sweeping the floors after they leave. Subversive service is more than a gesture for them; it has become a habit. They're not perfect and don't pretend to be, but they invest most of what they have in supporting a community of disciples. They try to give to those who ask. If you ask them why they live the way they do, they'll tell you they honestly can't imagine a better life.

But they'll also tell you that they still have questions about how God's people relate to this world of power. Pat is an estate lawyer, after all, the sort of guy who actually knows how to read a letter from the IRS. He makes a living interpreting the law as it relates to the property people own. Because he practices the tactics of Jesus, Pat knows firsthand the radical abundance of God's kingdom. But because he practices law, Pat also knows how this world works and how its authorities are threatened by people who don't share their assumptions. He knows the tension of trying to be "in the world but not of it."

When the United States first invaded Iraq in 2003, Pat thought it was the right thing to do. In a world where people do evil things, he considered it his country's moral obligation to get rid of Saddam Hussein. But as Pat heard stories from friends who had traveled to Iraq, he started to see what was happening there through the eyes of Iraqi Christians. He asked his community if they could start singing the refrain of Psalm 137 during morning prayers. They resonated with the cry of God's people in exile, and they committed to sing the psalm every day until the occupation of Iraq is ended.

"By the waters of Babylon, we lay down and wept," they sing. "We remember ... we remember ... we remember thee, Zion." Every morning a little community of disciples reminds itself of the tears their forebears cried in exile. Every morning they remember the vision they have to fix in their imagination when they become an alien in the land where they live. Pat says it helps them remember who they are.

The Claims
that Caesars Make

We don't live under Caesar anymore. We are the heirs of governments formed "of the people, by the people, and for the people," far removed from a time when emperors presented themselves as gods and exerted their wills on the populace. It's hard for most of us to imagine what it feels like to live under occupation. Even if we're just average citizens of the United States, we take comfort in thinking that we're part of a representative democracy. If we don't like the way things are, we can just wait four years and vote for new leadership.

At least that's what I was raised to think. But the U.S. invasion of Iraq in 2003 forced me to reimagine what it means to follow Jesus as a citizen of the world's last remaining superpower. When the attacks of September 11, 2001, happened, I was writing on faith and politics for a small webzine based in Philadelphia. As it became clear that our country was considering a war against Iraq, I started asking what resources the church had to think about war. I called a few Christian ethicists, found in a library the books they mentioned, and got a handle on the major traditions of just war and pacifism.

Pacifists say that Jesus taught and practiced non-violence and that it was the position of most Christians for the first three centuries. According to their tradition, violence is contrary to the way of Jesus, so Christians shouldn't fight. But pacifism is a minority position in most of church history. The majority position is the just war tradition. It says that there are times when love of neighbor compels us to use violence to keep some greater evil from happening. (It was necessary, for example, for a collection of nations to take out Hitler before he could conquer much of the world and finally eliminate the Jews.) The just war tradition has tried to develop criteria to determine when it is proper and needful for Christians to go into war and whether a particular war remains just once it is started. Logically, then, when a war is unjust Christians must refuse to fight in it.

When I felt like I had a broad understanding of these major traditions of Christian thought about war, I went back to the theology professors I had interviewed and asked them whether it would be just for the United States to invade Iraq. Almost everyone I talked to said no. (Every major denomination except the Southern

Baptists made a statement against invading Iraq before March of 2003.) Yet, when I visited the Pentagon in the fall of 2002 and talked to people who had their finger on the military's pulse, it was clear that the United States would invade in the next year, maybe sooner. Tens of thousands of Christians were poised to fight, and it seemed like there was almost no possibility that any significant number of soldiers would refuse. Even though the just war and pacifist traditions said there were good reasons for Christians to seriously question this particular war, Christians in America didn't seem very free to do anything other than toe the line. Life in a democracy suddenly looked a lot more like life under Caesar.

As U.S. citizens who had the freedom to travel (though we were sternly warned against it by our government), my wife and I decided to go to Iraq with the Christian Peacemaker Teams at the beginning of the U.S. invasion. After the bombing had already begun, we drove through Iraq's western desert to Baghdad. There we talked to people whose homes were hit by surgical strike missiles and visited hospitals to mourn with parents whose children had become "collateral damage." We heard a weeping father say, "If this is democracy, we don't want it." We cried with a mother who stood beside her daughter's hospital bed and showed us a picture of her son who didn't survive. When the bombs woke us up at night, we prayed with everyone else in Baghdad for the terror to end.

In the darkness of those long nights, as I felt the earth shake beneath me after every blast, it occurred to me that I had helped pay for those bombs. A tax-paying citizen of the United States, I had made my small contribution to the largest defense budget in the world. Whether I liked it or not, what I often referred to as "my money" was being used to shock and awe a city of millions in the middle of the night.

I thought about the buildings that are pictured on the back of U.S. dollars—buildings I had admired when I lived in Washington, D.C. They weren't unlike the Iraqi government buildings that were in flames across the river from our hotel room. But they represented a different kingdom—the United States where I was born. And they reminded me that *my* money isn't really *mine*. It's the legal tender of a government that demands my loyalty. Money ties us to a whole system of powers, and our money uses us as much as we use it. Caesar will get what's due him, you can be sure—but the problem is that Caesar is never satisfied. He asks for more and more until he demands our very lives.

Dwight D. Eisenhower, the heroic general of the Second World War who became president in 1953, warned America as he was leaving the White House about the formation of a "military-industrial complex" which seemed to have a life of its own. A political realist, he could see from experience what St. Francis had heard Jesus say: that you cannot amass great possessions without also having to take up the sword and defend them.

Looking back on the era that Eisenhower anticipated, John Perkins, a self-confessed "economic hit man" of the late twentieth century, has written,

> The corporatocracy is not a conspiracy, but its members do endorse common values and goals.... The lives of those who "make it," and their accoutrements—their mansions, yachts, and private jets—are presented as models to inspire us all to consume, consume, consume. Every opportunity is taken to convince us that purchasing things is our civic duty.... People like me are paid outrageously high salaries to do the system's bidding. If we falter, a more malicious form of hit man, the jackal, steps

to the plate. And if the jackal fails, then the
job falls to the military.[1]

Because the desires of the consumer and the military
are more or less the same, the two work together almost
seamlessly. It's no accident that while the United States
prepared for war after 9/11, President Bush publicly
called for Americans to go shopping. Our wars and our
money go hand in hand.

Given the economics of scarcity that we see in the
systems of this world, it's hardly surprising that broken
people with power would use violence to ensure their
own security and comfort. In a struggle for survival, the
strong survive by beating out the weak. It is heartbreaking, though, that Christians who should be investing in
God's economy so often join our culture of conspicuous
consumption with Jesus-brand products. It is even more
heartbreaking to see Christians praying God's blessing
on the bombing of foreign cities to protect our American way of life. We give in so easily to Caesar's claim on
human souls, failing to interrupt the assumptions and
demands of our military-industrial complex.

Jesus' question about the denarius points us to a
deeper question about who we are. "Whose image is
on the coin?" Jesus asks the Torah scholars who wanted

to catch him in his words. But Jesus identifies their hypocrisy in clinging to the dirty money of an occupying force that demands total allegiance. These religious leaders knew well the story of how God created humans "in his image," stamping us with the likeness of our Maker so that everyone would know whose we are. Caesar can stamp his picture on a piece of metal, Jesus says, but God's image is stamped on our very beings, and God has already claimed our allegiance. Our money belongs to the Treasury Department, and they can force us to give it back if they so desire, but our lives belong to God. Caesar can kill us, or demand that we kill, but our resurrected Lord lives as a reminder that the abundant life of God is stronger even than death.

Pledging Allegiance with Our Lives

Jesus' tactic of gracious politics is an invitation to practice resurrection in a death-bound society that offers few real options. In a political climate obsessed with simplistic either/or choices—"pro-choice" or "pro-life," hawk or dove, Republican or Democrat—Jesus invites us to disregard the accepted categories and pledge allegiance to God with our lives. Go ahead and give yourselves to the life God made you for, Jesus says, become the change God wants to see in the world. If someone sees some hope in the life you're living, invite them to join you. And if the authorities try to shut you down, don't worry. There is an empty tomb outside Jerusalem to remind us that Caesar's claims are limited.

A generation ago, when I was growing up, the Moral Majority movement in the United States successfully allied many Christians with the political right, saying that God was on the side of those who stood for family values and lower taxes. I don't doubt that Jesus also cares about families, money, the environment, and every other political hot-button issue—but I don't think he counts on the White House to do it. Instead, Jesus invites his children to give our lives to the gracious politics of living another way in the world.

I called Pat at Nehemiah House to ask him what he thinks it means to give Caesar what is Caesar's and God what is God's. "Well, all that I have is God's," Pat said to me. "I guess that doesn't leave much for Caesar. If he's going to come and take it, okay. But I'm going to use what I can while I have it for the kingdom." Pat told me about a program their community has started to provide affordable housing for single mothers and an extended family for their children as they try to get an education and find jobs. When one mother relapsed, abandoning her young daughter for the lure of drugs, Pat and Debbie became foster parents for the child. But they didn't give up on the mother, insisting that her daughter needed her and that she could come back and be a mother again when she got clean. They said they would help her get back on her feet, and they did. She and her daughter are living in the Nehemiah House community now, trying to be a healthy family in the midst of a new and beloved community.

I don't know whether Pat is "pro-choice" or "pro-life," but I know Nehemiah House is good news in a world where those positions are presented as either/or responses to abortion. Affirming the lives of mothers and children both born and unborn, this community of Christ-followers is also empowering women to choose for themselves a life that is truly life. They haven't figured out all the complexities of how to fix our broken society in the aftermath of *Roe v. Wade*, but they have engaged in gracious politics, showing their neighbors a better way. They're pledging allegiance to God with everything they have and watching to see what happens.

We need more of the creative politics that Jesus' tactical imagination inspires. From hospitals to prison reform, from abolition to care of the mentally ill, and from women's rights to civil rights, the lasting social change that God's followers have made possible throughout history has never been the result of a powerful church fixing things from the top down. In fact, God's followers have often had to work *against* a church that was too comfortable in the world's power structures. Change comes from the leavening effect of Christians' giving their lives on the ground, loving people who are outcasts, and proclaiming God's abundant economy. Our attempts to force people into the best life we can imagine have failed, but our efforts to celebrate the hospitality of God are contagious. A hungry world savors real signs of a better way.

In an essay entitled *The Christian Witness to the State*, church historian John Howard Yoder outlines a model for political engagement based on this historical observation and a conviction that Christians must distinguish between their "witness function and a self-seeking participation in the power struggle."[2] When I was struggling to recover from the allure of political power, Yoder's essay grabbed my imagination and gave me hope that another way is possible.

Yoder says Jesus is Lord of all, so the church should have something to say to governments. (In reaction against the Christian Right, I had been tempted to retreat into a separatist mentality.) When we witness to the state, though, Yoder insists that the "the centrality of the church's own experience must remain clear."[3] We tell the powers what we have seen and heard in the new humanity that God makes possible, but we don't have to answer every question society asks. Some of this world's questions make little sense to us once we've learned the ways of God's economy. (Why, after all, is "pro-choice" the opposite of "pro-life"? Can't we all decide to choose life?) But even if we reject the world's way of naming problems, the beloved community of God's family is not an otherworldly reality. Because we negotiate the same challenges that confront all people, the church can speak from its experience about what is possible.

Do we have anything to say about abortion? It seems to me that the folks at Nehemiah House do. A woman whose life is so broken that she would abandon her own child can recover to the point where she raises her daughter and values her own life. That's a story worth telling and one that lawmakers or social workers might learn from.

Does the church have anything to say about economic and foreign policy? We may, but not too quickly. We need to practice Jesus' first four tactics and learn their lessons well before we put too much energy into talking to the powers that be about what we've learned. After all, Jesus is clear in saying that the people who are invested in the world as it is won't like most of what we have to offer anyway. "If the world hates you, keep in mind that it hated me first" (John 15:18). The government executed Jesus as a subversive criminal, so we ought not be surprised if they don't want to listen to our gospel economics. But conversion is possible, and we are called to live in hope that nothing is beyond redemption — not even Wall Street or the White House.

Interrupting Business as Usual

Jesus' tactic of gracious politics is part of the public teaching he offers in the Temple courts just before his execution. Matthew, Mark, and Luke highlight the fact that before Jesus does any teaching in the Temple, he interrupts business as usual in that holy place. "On reaching Jerusalem, Jesus entered the temple area and began driving out those who were buying and selling there. He overturned the tables of the money changers and the benches of those selling doves, and would not allow anyone to carry merchandise through the temple courts" (Mark 11:15–16).

Practicing gracious politics under occupation, Jesus never tries to drive the Romans out. But he does drive the money changers out of the Temple, quoting the prophets Isaiah and Jeremiah: " 'My house will be called a house of prayer for all nations.' But you have made it 'a den of robbers' " (11:17).

Some contemporary Christians are filled with righteous indignation about the murderous violence that is committed "in our name" by leaders we elected. The bolder among us are sometimes inspired by Jesus and the prophets to perform symbolic acts of resistance against missile silos or military sites like the School of the Americas at Ft. Benning, Georgia, where counterinsurgents from Latin America have been trained in torture tactics that they have employed on church workers, missionaries, and poor farmers in their home countries.[4] The Romans of Jesus' day could be equally cruel, and I have no doubt that Jesus hated what they were doing. But our Lord reserved his prophetic interruption for the Temple — the place where God's people were supposed to be living an alternative to the madness of the world's system.

The text Jesus quotes about what the Temple ought to be comes from Isaiah's glowing vision of God's economy shining on a hill for all the world to see.

It's a passage that connects with the deep hunger we all share for something more than the life we know in a broken world. "Come, all you who are thirsty," the prophet sings. "Come to the waters; and you who have no money, come, buy and eat!" (Isaiah 55:1). God's new economy is good news for the poor—good news here and now for people who have been overlooked and neglected. And it is open to all, Isaiah says: "Let no foreigner who has bound himself to the Lord say, 'The Lord will surely exclude me from his people'" (56:3). No, Isaiah says with a flourish, celebrating the welcome of our Father's table: "My house will be called a house of prayer for all nations" (56:7).

But that is not what was happening at the Temple in Jerusalem, and it does not describe many of our churches today. Jesus was not surprised that Rome had bread only for those who could pay for it. That, he knew, was how the world's system worked. But Jesus was outraged that religious people would consort with the Empire in its violence and then use the Temple as their hideout. "Will you steal and murder, commit adultery and perjury," the Lord asks in Jeremiah, "and then come and stand before me in this house, which bears my Name, and say, 'We are safe'—safe to do all these detestable things?" (Jeremiah 7:9, 10). That's not the kind of security Jesus offers.

God is in the blessing business, for sure, but God blesses from within his economy of never-ending abundance, not from within our economy of wars, financial greed, and prideful personality contests. God has blessed us with the invitation to new life now, and Jesus will guide us into true abundance as we walk in his way. But he will not be used as a brand for our products. Jesus won't let his Father's house be a safe haven from the backlash we have coming if we collude with the world's sinful systems of money and power.

Jesus interrupts our attempts to marry God and Money under Caesar's banner. And if there is anywhere that the body of Christ needs to engage in symbolic action, it's in our houses of worship. "For it is time," as 1 Peter says, "for judgment to begin with the family of God" (4:17). I'm not suggesting that we go to other people's churches—"those" reprobate churches—and preach at them about what they're doing wrong. Rather, it seems Jesus' cleansing of the Temple is an invitation for us to lament how *we* in *our* churches have ignored the invitation to God's economy and endorsed the violence of this world's system. Maybe gracious politics in our time is about making our repentance public and tell-

ing a skeptical world that we have, in fact, been wrong.
But there's still hope—hope even for a broken church
in a messed-up world—because the God of abundance
invites us all to the table. The last word is always hope.

An Abundance
of Broken Pieces

Jesus' tactics for subverting this world's system with God's economy are good news for everyone. But they aren't easy teachings for most of us. Even the people who walked and talked with Jesus in first century Palestine struggled to imagine how they could receive the abundance they were invited into. The disciples left everything to follow Jesus, but God's economy was still hard for them to comprehend. Thankfully, Jesus didn't just teach tactics for a good life now. He invited the disciples to put them into practice and see God's abundance now.

In the ninth chapter of Luke's gospel, a crowd gathers to hear Jesus teach. All day long they've hung on his every word, and now it's getting late. "Send the crowd away," the disciples say, "so they can go to the surrounding villages and countryside and find food and lodging, because we are in a remote place here" (Luke 9:12). Bellies are rumbling. But resources are scarce, the disciples note. Defaulting to the realism of this world's economy, the disciples think the only way to meet the need is to send every person to fend for himself. Take the family to a restaurant. Grab a bite to eat on the trip home. Use what you have to provide for your own. It's the best solution they can imagine.

But Jesus says, "You give them something to eat." It's an amazing interruption—a jolting call for them to put their faith into practice. "If you believe in abundance, then let's see it," Jesus says. "Don't send the crowds away. The good news they've heard doesn't mean much until it becomes a reality they can see, a meal they can eat, a community where they can celebrate the abundance of their Father." Jesus refuses the logic of scarcity that every modern economy assumes. He knows that in his Father's world there is already enough for every need. In short, he insists on God's abundance.

But Jesus doesn't just hand the disciples bread to distribute to the masses. He doesn't give them anything. "*You* give them something to eat," he says (9:13, emphasis added). The abundance that Jesus wants the disciples to tap into is not a magical power that turns stones into bread. Jesus has already considered that option in Luke 4, when he was hungry himself after a forty-day fast. In the remote and barren desert, the devil tempted Jesus with the "name and claim it" doctrine: "If you are the Son of God, tell this stone to become bread" (Luke 4:3). But Jesus turned down the quick fix. He refuses to overwhelm our needs with miraculous provision. Jesus chooses, instead, to work a miracle through his weak and broken community.

The disciples point out to Jesus how little they have—fives loaves, two fish, and not nearly enough money to cater a meal for five thousand. What are they to do with so little in a world of such great need? "Have them sit down in groups of about fifty each," Jesus says (Luke 9:14). God's abundance is never ending, but needs are *limited*. The hungry are not infinite in number. This crowd can be broken down into fifties. I love it that Jesus doesn't ask the disciples to feed a crowd of five thousand. He invites them instead to bring what they have and trust God to provide for a hundred small groups.

It's still crazy, of course. One family's lunch isn't going to feed all those hungry people, no matter how you slice it. But Jesus takes what they have, gives thanks, and breaks it. He breaks up the crowd and he breaks up the meal. Then he sends the disciples around as waiters to serve each group. And after everyone has had their fill, Jesus sends them around again to collect the leftovers. "The disciples picked up twelve basketfuls of broken pieces that were left over," Luke says (9:17). I can imagine the twelve, each with his basket, shaking their heads in disbelief. How in the world did *that* happen?

I can't explain how it happened ... or how it happens. To trust the radical economy of God's abundance is to live by faith. But like the bread the disciples shared in the desert, the endless supply we trust is not a credit card without a spending limit or a food bank with shelves that are always fully stocked. The bread that feeds five thousand is an *abundance of broken pieces.*

It's hard to trust fragments, especially when we live amidst the material abundance of the most advanced economy the world has ever known. Strategies to end poverty and rid the world of hunger sound more effective than the tactics of Jesus. The promise of health and wealth—or at least a little piece of the American pie—can seem so much more appealing than a basketful of leftovers. It's hard to believe in an abundance of broken pieces.

But bread has to be broken to be shared. While the feast consists of bread and meat, the meal isn't a feast until it's celebrated with people we love. The banquet isn't what it was meant to be until the whole family has come.

Theologians tell us that God doesn't need anything. God was always complete in God's self and never lacked anything. But God chose to create. God chose to invite us into community with him. And the whole story of Scripture seems to say that God's party isn't finished until all his children are gathered around the table, breaking the bread we have, passing the pieces to one another, and living the beloved community that is communion with our Lord.

This journey I've been on since tripping over Jesus outside Union Station is, I've started to see, a journey into God's economy. It's a walk with Jesus that is, at the same time, a life in community. "Heaven is a banquet," Dorothy Day wrote, "and life is a banquet too, even with a crust, where there is companionship."[1] Maybe companionship is the life we were made for. Maybe that's what all our hungers point toward. Maybe that's the economy our world most desperately needs.

Maybe if we break what we have and share it, we can start living heaven's banquet now.

Acknowledgments

I couldn't have written a book on God's economy—and certainly wouldn't believe in it—if it weren't for the innumerable gifts of friends who showed me the way. My life happens and is sustained by the community at Rutba House. That y'all put up with a writer in the midst of everything else is a sign of how far we've grown into a culture of grace. Thank you. Leading the way and keeping us honest is our extended community in Walltown. A big part of that circle is our family at St. Johns Baptist Church, where Sunday dinner in the fellowship hall is a mighty fine picture of what heaven's banquet must be. Fried chicken and collard greens ... mmmm.

But, alas, nobody can eat all the time. So I'm grateful, too, for the walks, Isaac; for your thoughtful emails,

Kelly; for your encouragement, Marty; and for the conversations along the way, Shane. It's a great gift to work with Sarah, Sam, Tim, Maria, Scott, Evan, Chanequa, Amy Laura, and Eric on the School for Conversion (www.newmonasticism.org). Nobody gets paid what they're worth in this endeavor, which is a reminder that we're sharing gifts. Your generosity points me to God's economy. The community of communities that we work out of and celebrate is a good reminder that God's abundance is real enough to offer you a bed and a warm meal when you're away from home. Thanks for doing it again and again. And thanks for going public for the sake of shouting the good news with our lives. (To find a community near you, see www.community ofcommunities.us.)

After stumbling into writing, I'm glad to have found in Greg Daniel a partner who actually knows what he's doing. Thanks for helping me imagine this project and get clear on just what I was trying to say. Angela Scheff is the sort of editor who makes you sound better by helping you sound more like yourself. Thanks to you, Angela, and to you, Bob Hudson and Kathleen Merz, for taking to heart all the words you read so carefully. I'm grateful to all the folks at Zondervan who're taking the good news to places I'll never get to go.

Acknowledgments

Leah, you make my writing possible as a part of our life together by both trusting me to do this work and helping me remember the life and community it's meant to serve. By the time I've got something worked out enough to write it down, you hardly need to read it. But I take it as a vote of confidence that you send my books to friends in prison. I hope, someday, that this book will mean something to you, JaiMichael. In the meantime, thanks for loving stories like Pinocchio and asking me to read them to you one more time.

I was born into a generous family that has never stopped giving to me. Thanks Mom and Dad, Josh, Nana, Pa, Grandpa Hartgrove, Granny Bern, Pa Taylor, and everybody else (we've got a big family, and I don't want to forget anyone). Grandma Ann, you adopted us into a family bigger than I could have imagined. Day by day, you're teaching me to trust God's radical abundance. This book is dedicated to you, with gratitude.

Notes

Chapter 2: Hungry for More

1. Marva J. Dawn, *Powers, Weakness, and the Tabernacling of God* (Grand Rapids: Eerdmans, 2001), 5.

2. Mike Davis, *Planet of Slums* (London: Verso, 2006), 22–23.

3. Jacques Ellul, *Money and Power* (Downers Grove, Ill.: InterVarsity), 27.

4. Ibid., 28.

5. Ibid.

Chapter 3: Eating at God's Table

1. Mrs. Hamer's story is told in Charles Marsh, *God's Long Summer* (Princeton, N.J.: Princeton University Press, 1997), 18–22. See also Andrew Young's account in his interview with Vincent Harding, Veterans of Hope Project (www .veteransofhope.org).

2. See Marsh, *God's Long Summer.*

3. Robert Frost, "The Road Not Taken," in *Robert Frost's Poems*, ed. Louis Untermeyer (New York: Simon and Schuster, 1971), 223.

Chapter 4: Subversive Service:
How God's Economy Slips In

1. Arthur C. Brooks, "Does Money Make You Happy?" *The Christian Science Monitor* (June 24, 2008).

2. Quoted in G. K. Chesterton, *Saint Francis of Assisi* (New York: Doubleday, 1990), 56.

3. Peter Maurin, a popular teacher who worked out his ideas in memorized talks, wrote his arguments as Easy Essays that were printed as free verse poems in *The Catholic Worker* newspaper. This quote is from an Easy Essay entitled "A Question and Answer on Catholic Labor Guilds."

4. Kelly Johnson, *The Fear of Beggars: Stewardship and Poverty in Christian Ethics* (Grand Rapids: Eerdmans, 2007), 194.

Chapter 5: Eternal Investments:
How God's Children Plan Ahead

1. Robert Farrar Capon, *Health, Money, and Love: and Why We Don't Enjoy Them* (Grand Rapids: Eerdmans, 1990), 39.

2. I've written about new monasticism and my own journey into it in *New Monasticism: What It Has to Say to Today's Church* (Grand Rapids: Baker, 2008). For a description of the economic life of our communities, see chapter 6 in that book, "Daily Bread and Forgiven Debts," 89–105.

3. Richard B. Sewall, *The Life of Emily Dickenson* (Cambridge, Mass.: Harvard University Press, 1998), 23.

4. Paul Zane Pilzer, *God Wants You to be Rich: How and Why Everyone Can Enjoy Material and Spiritual Wealth in Our Abundant World* (New York: Touchstone, 1995), 173.

Chapter 6: Economic Friendship: How Real Security Happens

1. William Herzog, *Parables as Subversive Speech: Jesus as Pedagogue of the Oppressed* (Louisville: Westminster John Knox, 1994), 240. Herzog's social analysis of the parables in context has helped me to imagine how Jesus' audience might have heard the stories he told. Imagination being what it is, though, Herzog ought not be blamed for my speculation about what might be going on in this story.

2. James C. Scott, *Weapons of the Weak: Everyday Forms of Peasant Resistance* (New Haven, Conn.: Yale University Press, 1985), xvi–xvii. For a discussion of the distinction between "offstage" and "onstage," see 25–27.

3. Kai Wright, "The Subprime Swindle," *The Nation*, July 14, 2008.

4. Mohammed Abbas, "Islamic Banks Shielded from Subprime," Reuters News Service, *www.reuters.com/article/managerViews/idUSNOA43244920080204*. Accessed August 8, 2008.

5. Elliot Blair Smith, "Dream Fulfilled Helps Muslims Realize Theirs," *USA Today* (February 24, 2005). *La-riba* means "no interest" in Arabic. What a great name for a bank.

6. For more information about this health care co-op, see *www.christianhealthcareministries.org*.

Chapter 7: Relational Generosity:
How We Share Good News

1. Herbert McCabe, *The People of God: The Fullness of Life in the Church* (Lanham, Md.: Sheed & Ward, 1964), xi.

2. Albert Borgmann, *Power Failure* (Grand Rapids: Brazos, 2003), 103.

3. John Chrysostom, *On Wealth and Poverty*, trans. Catharine P. Roth (Crestwood, N.Y.: St. Vladimir's Seminary Press, 1984), 53.

4. Quoted in Mary Ellen Hombs, *Homelessness in America: A Forced March to Nowhere* (Washington, D.C.: Community for Creative Nonviolence, 1983), 121.

5. Clarence Jordan, *Sermon on the Mount* (Valley Forge, Pa.: Judson, 1993), 54.

Chapter 8: Gracious Politics:
How to Live Under Occupation

1. John Perkins, *Confessions of an Economic Hit Man* (New York: Plume, 2006), xv–xvi.

2. John Howard Yoder, *The Christian Witness to the State* (Newton, Kans.: Faith and Life Press, 1964), 55. Yoder outlines the form of the church's witness on pages 16–22.

3. Yoder, *The Christian Witness to the State*, 16.

4. See the School of Americas Watch, www.soawatch.org.

Epilogue: An Abundance
of Broken Pieces

1. Dorothy Day, *The Long Loneliness* (New York: Harper & Row, 1952), 285.

Mirror to the Church

Resurrecting Faith after Genocide in Rwanda

Emmanuel Katongole with Jonathan Wilson-Hartgrove

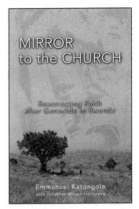

We learn who we are as we walk together in the way of Jesus. So I want to invite you on a pilgrimage.

Rwanda was often held up as a model of evangelization in Africa. Yet in 1994, beginning on the Thursday of Easter week, Christians killed other Christians, often in the same churches where they had worshiped together. The most Christianized country in Africa became the site of its worst genocide. With a mother who was a Hutu and a father who was a Tutsi, author Emmanuel Katongole is uniquely qualified to point out that the tragedy in Rwanda is also a mirror reflecting the deep brokenness of the church in the West. Rwanda brings us to a cry of lament on our knees where together we learn that we must interrupt these patterns of brokenness.

But Rwanda also brings us to a place of hope. Indeed, the only hope for our world after Rwanda's genocide is a new kind of Christian identity for the global body of Christ — a people on pilgrimage together, a mixed group, bearing witness to a new identity made possible by the Gospel.

Softcover: 978-0-310-28489-5

Pick up a copy today at your favorite bookstore!

Share Your Thoughts

With the Author: Your comments will be forwarded to
the author when you send them to *zauthor@zondervan.com*.

With Zondervan: Submit your review of this book
by writing to *zreview@zondervan.com*.

Free Online Resources at
www.zondervan.com

Zondervan AuthorTracker: Be notified whenever your
favorite authors publish new books, go on tour, or post
an update about what's happening in their lives.

Daily Bible Verses and Devotions: Enrich your life
with daily Bible verses or devotions that help you start
every morning focused on God.

Free Email Publications: Sign up for newsletters on
fiction, Christian living, church ministry, parenting, and
more.

Zondervan Bible Search: Find and compare
Bible passages in a variety of translations at
www.zondervanbiblesearch.com.

Other Benefits: Register yourself to receive online
benefits like coupons and special offers, or to participate
in research.

ZONDERVAN®
.com